HOOKED
on
HAPPINESS

J.Z. WOLFE

BAD APPLE
Los Angeles

DEDICATION

I would like to express my deepest gratitude to the many people who saw me through this book. To my mom, dad, sisters and brothers, friends, and expert editor who offered support, talked things over and allowed me to utilize them for their exceptional proofreading and editing. I am endlessly grateful for the publishing magic of Bad Apple. And of all those who have been with me over the years, thank you.

CONTENTS

CONTENTS

FOREWORD

You have everything you've ever wanted. Your needs are met daily and all things in life are going according to plan. And the best part is: you and the people around you recognize it. For the first time, nothing stands in your way.

But then *it* happens—an insatiable craving for *more*. This hunger cannot be satisfied. Most of us know what this looks and feels like. Even though things seem to be ideal, better than they've ever been before, our diet spins out of control, exercise is a chore, and there's endless self-doubt, anxiety, and worry kicking us further into this dangerous cycle.

You may think you're living the dream, but you still feel unhappy. No matter what, there's that little voice telling you how to think and feel, leaving you miserable!

Whether you're at the top of your game, like in the aforementioned scenario, or working toward your own brand of happiness, you might still end up in the same place—being unhappy.

The underlying factors of this phenomenon—being unhappy even though conventionally we should be happy—are often overlooked.

On the surface, we have the pursuit of happiness. It's often displayed as a drive to go after the things that should make us happy. It's a simple equation: seek the things you want *plus* get them and that *equals* happiness. Surprisingly, this does not appear to work every time for everyone.

It seems, especially in the United States, happiness is a relentless chase which has left many of us sad, tired, empty, and often lonely. We've been led to believe that happiness is just beyond our reach and all we have to do is go out and get it. Once we finally achieve even a small amount of bliss, we feel a sense of peace and accomplishment.

Yet there is always something newer, bigger or better we haven't yet tried. It's like running laps in a hamster wheel, continuously going in circles searching for the next big thing.

Then once we get to our goal, instantly, we're dashing toward the latest device, new trend or fad and the whole cycle of addiction begins again. It's this pursuit of happiness that gives us short-lived results. And is short-term happiness what we really want?

We may believe that we're above this cycle, but as many read this book their goal could be, "How can I *achieve* more happiness." Rather than, "How can I *be* happier." The key word is "be."

Be happier instead of wanting more.

There is an underlying factor more pervasive than the wild hunt which silently erodes our sense of happiness every day. It has caused a new era in our quest.

This major cause surrounding the pursuit of happiness is our addiction to it.

As defined by the American Society of Addiction Medicine (ASAM), "...Addiction is characterized by a...craving that [diminishes] the recognition of significant problems."[1]

It is then a desire which is satisfied through outside means. These actions can then lessen our realistic perceptions of the possible future damages and can cause major issues to arise in our lives. We can relate this definition to a compulsion toward feeling or not feeling (wanting more) happiness, as well.

It is not merely the greedy craving of it, but also the feeling and high of acquiring happiness. The sensations generated from achieving joy have a tremendous force. A reason for stopping at nothing to get more of what we want is, well, it feels good—really good.

When we're happy, things just seem to fall into place. The tingly sensation of accomplishment that undoubtedly puts a smile on our faces reduces the impact of negative emotions and experiences in our lives. Almost nothing can get us down. We may even see things through rose-tinted glasses. Happiness can make everyday events seem more satisfying and meaningful.

We are typically at our best when we're feeling happy. The added boost of chemicals pulsing through our brains and bodies (serotonin, dopamine, oxytocin and endorphin) can create what is often referred to as a "happy high."[2]

This high drives us to want more, get more and ignites a cyclical pattern to constantly search for bliss.

It's simple to recognize the addictive nature surrounding happiness. Look no further than your own life.

In our daily routines, we might go above and beyond to get a new house, job, car, expensive clothes, and the list keeps increasing. Sure we may feel the immediate high of happiness when we obtain these new things, but that might be short-lived, and they may not support our desire for long-term satisfaction.

It comes at us from all sides in movies, media, and even our doctors might spread the notion that we should and can be *continuously* happy. Many offer supplements, books, seminars, pharmaceuticals and more to feed our happiness addiction each year.

It seems to have developed beyond a simple pursuit and is now a national obsession. The results of this can be the exact opposite to our good intentions. It appears to have caused a nation of happy seekers to be, in fact, unhappy.

One in seven Americans, at some point, have had symptoms relating to depression. Shockingly, the number of people diagnosed increases almost 20% each year[3]

Even though we are given newer and better ways to get happier each year, the numbers do not lie. We're not always as happy as we'd like to be.

Happiness has become, after hundreds of years in the making, a consuming force. It is like any other obsession. We crave it, work toward it, and will basically stop at nothing until we have more of it.

Yet the most ironic part to this complex behavior is there is still much confusion and disagreement surrounding what happiness actually *is*. Today, our happiness—and unhappiness—have led us in the wrong direction, but that won't be the case for long.

CHAPTER ONE

So...what is happiness? Is it a feeling? Is it a mood? Is it a behavior?

There's a common belief that happiness is an emotion much like any other. The sensations that pulse through us when we're feeling good cause us to express ourselves in more positive ways. When we're feeling excited, we can seem more exhilarated, vibrant, and energized. All these characteristics did, in fact, start with the sensation of *feeling* happy.

As it turns out, though, happiness is more than a feeling. To those that acknowledge this and observe life satisfaction in this way are often referred to as happiness experts.

They research, catalog, and document everything about happiness—what it is, how it works, and the actions it inspires us to take. Some of their shared wisdom about living a happier life is to exercise three times a week, meditate, eat healthy food, and take up hobbies.

These practices often do, in fact, bring about a sense of joy and their research has shown to advance the prevention of depression and suicide helping many people create new and more fulfilling lifestyles. Naturally, this is what such behaviors are meant to do. Happiness experts know this. That's why most come out with new products, services, and routines each year to keep us striving to achieve more happiness.

But there remains one big problem: we often don't remain satisfied and, even worse, the expectation and pressure of being happy all the time is actually pushing us deeper into unhappiness.

Often we have no idea how to find a real sense of lasting joy. Our confusion can be broken down into two parts. The first is that happiness is represented as a one-size-fits-all, and second, the steps suggested in the past toward cultivating a more fulfilling life have been vague.

Happiness portrayed as one-size-fits-all often is presented as mass techniques, practices, or products which essentially casts a wide net that may not work well for every individual.

For example, the "Think Positive" movement promotes the concept that if we think good thoughts, then we can be happy, wealthy, and healthy.

In reality, though, solely relying on positive thinking can cause more harm than good and we may not see the reality of our situations. The belief that if we think differently we can change our lives and be happier is simply not the case.

Actually, if negative thinking or feeling negative in the face of bad experiences suits you, then you should do so because it creates a better quality of life—one in which you are true to yourself.[1] This, over time, can promote more of a sustainable sense of satisfaction.

The think positive technique can be frustrating in this way because we might feel we're not allowed to feel bad even though we ought to.

Let's hypothetically say someone is driving home from a bad day at work and they're thinking things like, "I hate this traffic," or, "my job is awful," or, "I can't stand my boss," then *bam*! They get into a car accident.

Was the accident caused by their negative thoughts? The resounding answer should be, "No."

So why do we eat up books, seminars and techniques that say just the opposite?

Positive thinking is often presented as a "one-size-fits-all" technique which cannot solely bring more happiness or good things into our lives and the opposite, negative thinking, won't necessarily bring us back luck.

Positive thinking promoted as an activity for everyone (a one-size-fits-all approach) could have results...and said results may vary. Not everyone can, or will, receive the same benefits.

We are all chemically, physically, and emotionally different and therefore will completely respond to exciting and negative situations in totally unique ways. Mass happiness techniques may adequately fit some, but it doesn't fit anyone well.

This pushes us, more often than not, into an unhappy cycle with many techniques that often do not work exclusively on their own.

Another reason for our confusion surrounding happiness is that in the past, the actions and steps suggested to finding happiness and sustaining it have been vague, misleading, and generalized.

Acquiring more of the things we want is one activity which is popularly promoted as making us happier. However, having more does not equate to living it up more. Similar to consuming more food, buying more clothes, homes, cars, or more things in general. These tangible objects do not mean you will have a fuller life.

We may think we're not caught up in this confusion, but consider this: when was the last time you checked your email?

For some, it's right when they wake up and for others it's an all-day activity. Now reflect on how many promotional emails you receive persuading you to "have more" in a given day. It could be enough to never give out your email address again.

The pressure to have the latest merchandise is constant and we can sometimes get caught up in the allure of new things. The expectation we feel is to go out and get the things that should make us happier. This continuously feeds the hunger which ultimately does not nourish our individual happiness.

This simple example illustrates that although we may feel we're not confused by happiness, we truly and often are.

This is a two-part challenge: one-size-fits-all and vague steps have both promoted our obsession toward what we think will bring us satisfaction, but instead has created a compulsion to sustaining our *happy high*.

That's exactly what we are regularly led to believe. If pure happiness can be related to a drug, then we'll stop at nothing to get more of it.

J.Z. WOLFE

CHAPTER TWO

Like any addiction, judgment can become clouded.
Optimism, the kind that is pervasive, constant and compulsive
can be more than just damaging, addictive, and unrealistic, but
can be a sign of impaired brain function.

Dr. Tali Sharot, a leading neuroscientist, and Professor Ray
Dolan, together with Christoph Korn, show that people who are
overly optimistic about everything could be working from faulty
frontal lobes.[1]

During their study, participants first filled out a questionnaire
measuring their optimism levels on a scale of high to low. After
they completed the assessment, the volunteers went through an
MRI scan to record brain activity.

They were given eighty negative life events such as car theft,
Parkinson's disease and cancer and then asked how likely these
events would occur in their lifetime. After a short break, the
researchers revealed the true and average probability of each
negative situation catered to the individual.

This gave the participants time to compare their first answers
to actual national averages. They were then asked a second time,
with this new information, how likely these events would occur in
their future.

There was a clear divide.

The participants with low to average optimism slightly adjusted their original estimates. For example, if the participant had foreseen their likelihood of suffering from cancer at 40%, but the average was 30%, then they might adjust their estimate to 35%—a marginal improvement with a realistic future prediction.

But if the information was worse than expected, the more optimistic participants tended to lower their original estimates. For example, if they were told the average for suffering from cancer was 30%, then they would decrease their estimate to 10% or even lower. Effectively ignoring the data altogether.[2]

The researchers also noted that when the data was considered "worse," the more optimistic participants showed little to no activity in the frontal lobes (also known as prefrontal cortex which is responsible for decision-making and future predictions) as if the brain waves were being interrupted or faulty.

To further demonstrate, in a related study, Dr. Sharot and her team introduced a small magnetic pulse at the frontal region of the brain impairing function. The results were the same, unrealistic and biased predictions of future events.[3]

It is then hypothesized that overly optimistic people might have faulty functioning frontal lobes which make it difficult for them to judge their future the way most of us do. They may disregard potential harm because they're hearing and seeing what they want and doing what they like.

This apathy, whether trained or biological, could put someone on the wrong side of happiness and result in a life that may move toward a dissatisfactory future.

Dr. Sharot refers to this as *optimism bias*, the ability to disregard real and potential future risks, a phenomenon which has baffled scientists for decades.[4]

However, Dr. Sharot explains this as a double-edge sword, "In general, optimistic people tend to be happier...[lowering] stress and anxiety, leading to better health and well-being." Though she warns, "However, [it] can also result in negative events since too-positive assumptions can lead to disastrous miscalculations."[5]

But how do we become overly optimistic, or happy in general?

According to Dr. Sharot, optimism is related to our brain's tendency to spend more time thinking of ways to successfully avoid bad events that may occur.[6]

More complexly, it's a combination of our brains, genes and experiences as she explains, "Experiences, in life, will alter how likely our brains are to function in an optimistic way." But our genes play a role as well, and "there is evidence suggesting that specific genes are related to optimism...[Thus] nature and nurture interact."[7]

Dr. Sharot concludes that we need to have a healthy balance of both optimism and realism to be happy. We need to realistically assess our weaknesses and strengths, as well as engage in experiences, activities and situations that build our optimistic outlook. This can lead to healthier lifestyle choices and brain function.

In truth, we're neither built to be constantly happy, nor should we be. If you think you should be happy all the time, it can be the slippery slope leading to a unhealthy obsession with happiness.

We may view overly optimistic people as the poster child for what bliss is. Yet happiness is not a constant and unrelenting sensation. It is a combination of many different factors, all unique and different to each lifestyle and person. We should not hold ourselves to such high happiness standards. The result from this stereotype and benchmark may result in disappointment.

This boils down to a question we should ask ourselves. How did we get to a place in time where happiness is a relentless and continuous pursuit, when modern science knows better?

Although we could immediately jump into our next actions and figure out what would bring a sense of lasting happiness into our lives, it's worth taking a step back. In fact, we should take many millennia steps back and turn to the past.

Without understanding the great transformations the concept of happiness has taken throughout history, we may be working from mistaken concepts about what happiness is for us now and how we'll later define it. To understand any obsession, we should go directly to the source of it.

CHAPTER THREE

Although the concept of happiness is alive and well today, it was once a perception reserved only for the lucky few who had the advantage of wealth, status, and hierarchy.

As we'll see, the ultimate beginning of happiness sets the tone for our insatiable addiction to it.

No matter how we move through this quick version of history, we'll recognize we've pushed, stepped over and deeply desired for a concept which has changed greatly over time.

Happiness has a rich history, a history that has significantly changed over the millennia. Yet, it seems, the main drivers for contentment have been consistently considered the pursuit of a goal that's always out of reach.

As early as the fifth century BCE, Herodotus wrote *The History*, one of the first works of antiquity in the West, in which Croesus, the king of Lydia, believes he is the happiest man.[1]

Although he does not write the word *happiest*, Herodotus uses other terms such as *oblios*, from the era of Homer and Hesiod, meaning "blessed" to describe heroes and gods having affluence.[2] The word blessed can be related to the word happy as it was seen as one of the highest hierarchical levels an individual could achieve at the time. Happiness was then seen as a rarity amongst everyday ancient people and a feature of fate.

A person had to be considered blessed to be happy and this set the tone for not only the rest of history, but also how we would ultimately define, pursue and obtain happiness in our current lives.

At the same time, the world's political and historical climate was unpredictable. Sickness was in almost every town. Children commonly died before adulthood; life was tolerated, but rarely enjoyed.[3]

For most, the concept of joy did not easily penetrate into the fabric of their daily lives. Life was hard with little luxuries or accommodations. Happiness, or a concept of happiness, was fleeting and not reserved for anyone who was not wealthy or had upper class status.

Our contemporary sense of happiness would have been a cruel joke in antiquity. Being happy was being blessed by fate and was primarily based on chance and reserved for the elite. If wealth or hierarchy blessed you, then you may have felt a small sense of joy. Everyone else was literally out of luck.

This created a word pattern that reflected the intangibility of happiness. In every European language—late Middle English and Middle Dutch—the word for happiness was derived from the word "luck."[4]

For example: Darrin M. McMahon, the author of *Happiness: A History*, points out in Middle English, the root of happiness is *happ*, meaning "chance," and related to "happens" or "happenstance."

In French, *bonheur* translates to "happiness" and is derived from *bon*, meaning "good," and the old French *heur* meaning "luck." Literally, meaning "good luck."

In Greek, the word *eudaimon* means "good fortune" and "god." Examples such as these are reflected in many languages throughout history, and all share the dialectal root for happiness as luck *and* fate.[5]

Our early sense of happiness was considered uncontrollable, predestined and random. It was up to fate or fortune and was something that happened to you if you were lucky and not something you could plan for or influence.

Yet, with the arrival of Greece's Golden Age (500 to 300 BC) came a new definition of happiness—being happy did not happen by chance; instead it was a trait.

Happiness was the outcome of living a virtuous life and engaging in good moral conduct. But it wasn't just doing good deeds that guaranteed you lasting happiness. It was considered a character trait to be virtuous, rather than an activity.

In Aristotle's seminal *Nicomachean Ethics*, one of the first studies on human well-being, he explains a virtuous person is righteous; therefore they will engage in good conduct, making them feel happy, and this virtuous state varied from person to person.[6] Both virtue and happiness were then individual traits and connected.

Around the end of the Middle Ages (1301–1500 AD) and early Renaissance (1401–1500 AD), people began to believe that they had the power to change their outside circumstances such as their governments, living conditions and even themselves, and then they could be happy.[7]

This was the beginning of what we are going to call the *transformation of happiness*. Happiness emerged as something completely attainable. But changing our surrounding circumstances to allow us to find what we seek—as we all know— is easier said than done.

Although ancient people were eager and ready to feel a greater sense of satisfaction, the concept of joy was still very vague and reserved for only the elite few.

Everyone could, in a sense, be happy, yet only the fortunate few were actually happy. For most, being happy was beyond their social and economic means. Feelings of oppression was more the norm. The political and economic climate again shaped the emerging concept of happiness.

From 1346–1665, the bubonic plague killed 30–60% of the population of Europe.[8] Those who didn't die faced famine or other hardships following the collapse of their societies. Simply put, most were unhappy and the happy few became even fewer.

Gradually, the frustration that happiness was only reserved for a select few was beginning to be felt and written about by the majority.

History takes another sharp turn when French literature and the Enlightenment movement asserted that happiness was for all. Documenting happiness as a real and tangible concept that was not reserved only for a few lucky people, but for everyone.

The Declaration of the Rights of the Man and of the Citizen of 1789 proclaims "the happiness of all" was for everyone.[9]

With the American (1775–1783) and French (1789–1799) revolutions, which marked the end of Enlightenment, happiness was redefined as a widespread motivation possible by all.

An intellectual tradition handed down from Herodotus through Aristotle was being challenged. Instead of happiness being fate, luck or a character trait, it became seen as achievable by the masses.

Though, the real game changer came in the form of the *Declaration of Independence*.

It seems, especially in the West, happiness, from this point on, takes on a whole new concept and ultimately becomes one of the singular definitions and pursuits throughout history. Happiness moved to being a pursuit that was and still is just beyond our reach.

Approximately 240 years ago in 1776, the United States' goal of happiness was firmly accepted with the Declaration of Independence which affirmed the pursuit of happiness was as important as life and liberty.

It was decreed that all people, in all places, should have the opportunity and the unalienable right, at minimum, to try to be happy.

This right ultimately encouraged all people, all over, with every fabric of their being, to pursue happiness. And so the *pursuit of happiness* as a driver of mainstream culture was born.

The Manifest Destiny (1845) rode the coattails of the Declaration of Independence. This was a widely held belief that American settlers were destined to develop their merits and remake America.

An irresistible destiny to accomplish this essential duty took root—only encouraging happiness to spread throughout the entire continent and beyond.[10]

Historian Frederick Merk remarks Manifest Destiny was born out of "a sense of mission to redeem the Old World by high example...generated by the potentialities of a new earth for building a new heaven."[11]

Some historians believe our new fondness for happiness was partly due to an aspect of history which never receives the credit it deserves.

In the mid nineteenth century, improved dentistry from the eighteenth century meant better teeth and was thought to have encouraged people to smile more often.

With more happy expressions came more feelings of joy. Guillaume Duchenne discovered, the muscles used in genuine smiling, called the "Duchenne smile" (1862), a smile with half open eyes and mouth turned up, was tied to the workings of emotions.[12]

This notion is supported by present research: the act of smiling, genuine or not, can make us feel happier.[13] Better teeth from dentistry and the discovery of genuine smiling, even if it seems like a small addition to history, meant more happiness.

Still happiness was a vague concept that many understood was attainable, yet did not know how. This confusion bled into the time period between 1914–1945 where happiness took a firm hold in pop culture as reflected in the music of the time.

An example is in the WWI song, "It's a Long Way to Tipperary." The lyrics declared: "All the streets were paved with gold/ So everyone was gay!"[14]

Also, in a WWII song, "We'll Meet Again," with the lyrics: "Tell them I won't be long/ They'll be happy to know."[15] This showed that happiness was beginning to resemble a sensation. Including the song "White Cliffs of Dover," with the lyrics, "There'll be love and laughter and peace ever after/ Tomorrow when the world is free."[16] This also reflected the importance of feelings associated with happiness.

History significantly pivots again when pop culture finally saturated mainstream Western culture enough that people wanted clear directions to happiness.

James Truslow Adams formulated a clear path to it by popularizing the idea of the "American dream," (1931) with roots in the Declaration of Independence, in which everyone deserved a chance to prosper and be happy as long as they worked hard.[17] This became the sounding board for the pursuit of happiness.

Unfortunately, though, this did not answer all the questions surrounding happiness, as working hard can be interpreted in many different ways. Although most felt they could be content, how to actually *be* happier remained a mystery.

It seemed our pursuit of happiness was like a treasure map with a large "X," but one that had no familiar landmarks.

Today, more than ninety years later, many feel their hard work and pursuit has reaped an unequal reward.

The Occupy Wall Street movement in 2011, whose slogan was "We are the 99%," implied that the United States is often controlled by the elite, the one percent. It tried to expose social and economic inequality conditions that run counter to the ideals of the American Dream, and frankly, happiness.[18]

It seems the pursuit of happiness and the concept of the America Dream has hit some hurdles.

At first we denied happiness by defining it as luck, fate and fortune. Then happiness was a virtuous trait. Either we had it or not. It transformed once again to being for everyone, but not everyone had the luxury to have it.

Then it was our natural state and an attainable right and a thing we were meant to pursue. Today, being happy is not only our natural state, choice, pursuit and compulsion, but, rightfully, no one can keep us from trying to be happy.

Throughout our many millennia-long concept of happiness, we have either denied ourselves it or wholeheartedly pursued it. This quest of happiness resembles more of a national obsession— an addiction—than a history.

Therein lies the challenge; after centuries of writing about, talking about and pursuing happiness, we still don't really know what happiness *is*, despite that its pursuit has captivated people all over the world.

Begging the ultimate assertion: the pursuit of happiness is not enough.

We have to strive for bigger. Instead of chasing a vague concept of happiness defined by all, we need to define and find individual happiness, one which is not centered on a lifestyle change, but instead looking within.

It's time to break the cycle and stop pursuing a senseless dream—bridging on a national addiction. It's time to find your own kind of happiness and exactly the way it is for who you are as an individual.

We must find our baseline happiness, and nothing more or less. This is who we are when we change nothing about our lives and represents our true selves.

Our baseline happiness is combination of realism and optimism. Also, its foundation is built upon our individual biology, psychology, emotions and environments. Uncovering our baseline happiness is discovering and defining happiness in our own way and at our own pace.

In this book, our obsession with happiness will be debunked

through a simple road map, with plenty of guidance along the way.

Everything we need is already available to us, but if we try to use the traditional and generic approach to pursuing happiness, we'll likely fail. Success is recognizing that our happiness is as individual as we are.

No one arrives at happiness purely by chance. You don't receive the benefits of lasting happiness without taking specific actions. Happiness is both a journey and destination that is created and supported by knowledge, communication and actions.

Given a chance, happiness will grow and, if nurtured, it can thrive. And if the joy you cultivate is your own, it will last.

The three ways to break the cycle and find your exclusive happiness starting today are: *know, tell, do.*

Know what makes you happy, tell others what makes you happy, and then do what makes you happy.

No longer will the question of what happiness is be a mystery, nor will it be unsustainable. Now there are defined actions to personal satisfaction.

It's time to discover your happiness. Your first action to breaking the unhappiness cycle is to get to know yourself on a whole new level.

CHAPTER FOUR

Before you bust out your top ten things that bring a smile to your face, hold on because you could be selling yourself short if we pass up the initial action to happiness—knowing yourself.

People who know themselves on a deep level are happier.[1] Period.

However, knowing ourselves goes beyond our likes and dislikes, our strengths and weaknesses; it's understanding why we do what we do and becoming aware of everything—the good, the bad, and the ugly.

We should *completely* know ourselves to receive a total view of our true self, happiness, and break our unhappiness cycle.

In the chapter before, a brief excerpt of history, helped us understand the root and progression of happiness for all. Now we will do the same for ourselves. Understanding our own happiness history, slowly uncovering more about ourselves, we will be able to form a solid foundation where our satisfaction can grow.

You will learn more about yourself than you ever thought possible and you'll find many competing traits and thoughts that are contrary to who you thought you were.

Conflicting behaviors can coexist within everyone and, ultimately, we may have opposing traits and thoughts which make up our true selves. Of course we might not like all of them and we don't have to because we are uncovering it all, not just the parts we like.

It could seem trivial to list all the ways we identify with the world and ourselves, but having this foundation will quickly catapult us into defining our personal and lasting happiness.

To become happier, we will analyze our true self—whoever that may be—and then make a decision about which direction we want to go.

The self is based on our genetics, the things that are predetermined, and our experiences which are often varied. Our genes can influence our experiences, and our experiences may or may not bring out our genetic predispositions. In an earlier chapter, Dr. Sharot shared that happiness is both nurture *and* nature.

An example of how our genes play a role in our experiences is why we freeze when confronted by danger.

Animals do react with the same behavior and this is because of the *amygdala* region in the brain (which humans also share) that regulates the processing and memory of emotions, fear and reactions. This part of the brain is, in many ways, considered primitive in its function. If trigged, you will freeze like any other creature.

When a tragic and sudden event happens (like 9/11 Twin Towers of the World Trade Center) most people freeze. This reaction is hardwired, but why?

It's speculated that predators are excited by movement and keeping still is often the best way to stay alive.[2] Freezing when feeling threatened is then innate.

However, some individuals when faced with the same danger will respond differently. The reason is that they've learned from experience to overcome their biology. For example, the rescue team that would assemble to assist after a catastrophic event does not let their hard-wired nature stop them—they've been trained to act.

If they had had no experience or training on how to react they too might inertly freeze waiting for danger to pass. Freezing when faced with danger is one of our most overt genetically determined traits.

Experiences can also play a role in how we act in our daily lives. Let's say you're naturally an introvert, a trait that is genetically and experientially rooted. This trait can sometimes rule your actions, thoughts, and even your relationships, and could result in different life experiences than someone who is considered extroverted.

It may seem, then, that altering your traits could fast track you toward happiness. Though that is not the case. It's not about changing yourself, but instead knowing more about who you are and what makes you—your true self—individually happy.

There will always be parts of ourselves that we wish we could alter. Like the pursuit of happiness, our chase of a better self-image is never ending and addictive. And as with any obsession, going outside of ourselves is something that might not be sustainable over time.

When we strip away everything, down to the core, what are we left with? Usually, the traits that we find most important in life.

Some identifiers are standardized (aspects that are obvious and often the same for many). While others, are more latent and unique. For example: a standardized identifier would be, "I am a woman." A more unique quality would be, "I am a female business owner." Overt identifiers are often recognizable at first sight. While our individuality is more than likely under the surface.

All this makes up who we are today and this person can be broken down into four parts. Each part is important to self-discovery and they are also significant to uncovering your unique sense of happiness:

1. The Me Self
2. The Secret Self
3. The Invisible Self
4. The Unseen Self

1.   The Me Self

This part shouts, "This is *me*, world!" It's definitive and often concrete, obvious and easily classified. The Me Self is known to you *and* known to others.

For instance, I am a woman. Or I have green eyes. Or I am six feet tall. It is often generic and biological and recognized to be true by most people.

Overall, The Me Self is important to our happiness, yet it can be deceiving. It's outwardly facing and consequently the largest part of our public selves which identifies us to the world. Though, it can be a slippery slope. We could get caught up in self-damaging thoughts, behaviors and acts to alter our self-image.

A word to the wise—how we come off to others can eventually alter our identity. For instance, if our friends believe we are short, even though we feel tall, this can over time cause us to think differently and negatively toward ourselves.

So recognize this as a part of your overall self. Not the whole deal. This is not the only aspect you will focus most of your growth on; it's only the beginning.

2.   The Secret Self

Bottling up all your feelings? Keeping it all in until you want to literally pop? Sound familiar?

This is the part of our identity, which is often the hardest to face, but it does not have to be negative. It is an excellent starting point to uncovering your true self.

The Secret Self is the part that is deeply known by you *but* unknown to others. It is everything we keep inside and is important to our self-discovery and happiness. Thus shedding new light on the things we may not want to face.

The saying, "We all have secrets," couldn't be truer in reference to this part, but some secrets are worth bringing to the surface. It's like lifting a heavy weight off our shoulders.

Examples of this part could be that we binge-watch sappy romance movies until dawn or we smoke cigarettes when we feel anxious.

Whatever it is, good or bad, it's intentionally or unintentionally building an identity which could influence our overall well-being.

We can start to chip away The Secret Self to get down to the bottom of ourselves—who we really are and how we came to be.

Our Secret Self can primarily be seen a sacred place within us we hold close. Having a protected "internal space" is significant and not sharing everything, with everyone, allows us to dive inward without outside influence.

Modern terms used for this perspective is our "gut" or "intuition." The Secret Self, if developed, can guide us and be a positive force in our lives.

Though, the opposite can be true as well. If The Secret Self is left to its own devices and is under developed, it can be damaging to our identity. Instances of this are bottling up negative emotions, not speaking up for ourselves when we should, or snapping at people because we feel pushed into a corner too often.

To get a grip on this part, we can simply start by uncovering it. This might be uncomfortable at first, but the payoff is significant.

Pick a secret, any secret, and start there. We are not going to be our own therapist or go out of our way to change the secret we find. Instead we are only uncovering our secret(s). This can be the most uncomfortable part.

For example, one of our secrets could be, "I'm still in love with an ex," or, "I'm on social media all the time at work," or, "I'm ashamed of my past." Or, "I desperately want to start a family one day." Once we have a couple professions, keep them in mind.

We are not changing ourselves or altering The Secret Self, we're developing it—that's all.

Recognizing and acknowledging your secrets and how they might be shaping your identity and happiness is the first step. This will gradually allow you to see yourself in a new light.

After you've hashed out a few secrets, said them out loud or thought about them clearly, you have placed them in the open and have successfully began to uncover your Secret Self. The next action is to allow it a place to thrive.

Allow your Secret Self to have a voice. If you have a situation that's bothering you, then it is your responsibility to acknowledge it. Or if you have a regret that is eating you alive, then you can take time to get quiet, think, write in your journal, meditate, or anything you need to do to release your bad feelings.

Your Secret Self can consume you if you let it. Allowing your thoughts and feelings to come and go, like an ocean wave, is learning how to be true to yourself. Having this attitude of giving your regrets space to breathe, rather than bottling up your emotions, will make you into a much happier person.

You can either be a person who has secrets that erode their relationship with themselves and others or you can be someone who positively identifies with themselves. The choice you make is related to how well you can "get comfy" with your innermost workings. Then you can have a life that is focused on true well-being.

We should and will have parts of ourselves which are kept secret. Keeping some things private, yet fully expressing ourselves, helps develop this part over time. Encouraging us to stand up for ourselves, voice our opinions, and make better decisions.

This part is our source of internal power, so take your time diving in and peeling back the layers. Finding the perfect balance between keeping it to yourself and wholeheartedly expressing yourself to the world.

3.   The Invisible Self

The Invisible Self is like venturing into uncharted territory. Often this self is difficult to understand and uncover because it's unknown to you *and* unknown to others. Classically referred to as the "subconscious" to access this hidden part is tricky, but not impossible.

There are actions you can take to uncover this part. Primarily, recognizing it as a possible influencer, we can start to debunk its mysteries. Though the ways in which we will proceed might seem unconventional.

Daydreaming and/or dreaming are often related to this part. What we see, feel, think and believe when we are not conscious could be indicators of our internal desires.

This part is subjective. What we choose to believe and move forward with is totally up to us.

If fully understanding your deep desires, dreams and thoughts is something you believe will not bring you closer to happiness then the next section can be viewed as knowledge sharing. Though, if you're ready to take the plunge, read on with an open mind.

Many individuals start and regularly write in journals. Taking note of wants, needs and reactions while awake or asleep can help improve memory and understanding our deepest aspirations.

Some even have *dream journals* where they catalog their nightly slumber. Our dreams, during sleep, can be an indication of how we are feeling or viewing ourselves in the waking world. Though there are many apps and blogs explaining the true meaning of dreams, it is a personal process.

For instance, if we consistently daydream we are on a beach, then that does not necessarily mean we have unresolved feelings of loss. It could simply mean we need a vacation. So be cautious about reading too much into anything or taking one source too seriously. A daydream or sleeping dream could be a modest spark of inspiration and motivation.

Though, if you want extra support in uncovering this part, you could seek a hypnotherapist. A hypnotherapist can assist with revealing the unconscious influences that can negatively or positively rule your life by using a technique called *hypnosis* (the process of putting someone into a deep state of relaxation to reveal hidden pains, desires, forgotten memories etc.) Over time their treatment can uncover a variety of subconscious triggers that could be effecting your well-being.

Whether you decide that seeking a professional is the best course of action or you would like to do this on your own, is up to you.

Your subconscious is there for a reason. It is an invaluable source for you to pull from and can tap into to uncover a possible path to joy. The Invisible Self is yours, and ultimately you are the keeper and decipher of its messages.

Creativity could spin off from your Invisible Self, urging you to take charge and expand your horizon. This is important to your overall happiness—to be inspired every day. And often this innovativeness could come to you in a relaxed state.

If we are to get hit by a lightning bolt of inspiration, it is in our best interest to investigate. It could lead us to a happier self where The Invisible Self is being fully expressed.

4.   The Unseen Self

The Unseen Self is the part that's totally unknown to you, *but* known to others. You could be thinking there aren't many things you don't know about yourself. Though you may be surprised.

It'll become quickly apparent we do not know as much as we thought we did about ourselves.

Without your knowledge, you could do things like curl your upper lip when you concentrate, when you drive you hum, when you are in an argument you pace, or crack your knuckles loudly.

These may or may not resonate with you, yet everyone has more than one thing they do instinctively and it has become habitual to the point they no longer notice it.

Your baseline happiness, the stuff we are when we change nothing, is fundamentally rooted in our unconscious habits. Those seemingly simple actions could be adding up to the culprit behind our lousy cycle.

Let's say you know someone who walks out when they get upset. They completely shut down and you can't get a word in.

Often, this behavior is referred to as "stonewalling." At first, it might not seem like a big deal because the person is doing it unintentionally. Though, it can be destructive to the other person's and their well-being.

It is damaging to walk out when upset because things never get resolved. Then the issue has the potential to be recurring. Walking out becomes a mechanism for the other person to use when backed into a corner.

Shutting down in a disagreement or doing any activity unconsciously is eroding your sense of happiness. If you continue to do things unknowingly then getting to know yourself and your joy will become increasingly more difficult.

The best way to approach The Unseen Self is to first, be ready for the unexpected. After all, we may learn some interesting facts which could be almost comical or corky.

Reflect on the new awareness you gain from this part. Do not go immediately into action-hero-mode and try to fix it. Let it marinate for a day, a week, a couple weeks, before altering it further.

The purpose of this process is to, again, not change what we find, only explore it. Often many things we find will eventually lead us toward a happier lifestyle. And on the flip side, there could be behaviors or reactions that could hinder us from a life worth living.

For now, however, let's take a leap outside of ourselves and get to know The Unseen Self. The only way to do this is to ask your friends, family and/or significant other.

The people closest to you have been watching you for a long time and their observations are central to revealing more of what you do habitually. When you can bring a sense of awareness to something, anything, that you are performing on "auto-pilot," you can foster a better self-image and life.

This can get messy, fast. So you'll need an arsenal of tools at your disposal before entering this unpredictable area of the self.

The Tools in Your Tool Belt:

- A healthy sense of humor
- An open mind
- Respect for the other person
- Something chocolate within arm's reach

Perfect. We're ready. Take a deep breath and find someone you trust. This is the most important and crucial step in developing The Unseen Self—to meet with someone you share mutual respect.

You could easily strike up a conversation with someone you are not too fond of, but their opinion may not be of value to you and tossed in the wastebasket. Realistically, you would get nothing out of the experience.

Asking someone you trust gives you a head start on this process. What they might have noticed about you could be funny, unique or embarrassing. Having someone you trust can help soften the truth.

Once you've selected this person, you can open up the conversation with, "We've known each other for a long time and can I ask you something?" Or, "I know you're great at noticing everything I do, so..."

Asking a question rather than making a statement eases a

tough conversation and gives it an "air of openness." Even if we're dying on the inside, they are there to help us become happier. So, clench those teeth, and continue. It gets better because understanding our little quarks, behaviors and actions we do unconsciously will give us a better sense of our true self and happiness.

Then when we do something again that we've learned is caused by us being in an "auto-pilot" mode, we can have an "Oh, I see" moment.

It could be the same as having an out of body experience. We can see ourselves through someone else's vantage point even if that means, momentarily, looking at ourselves in not the best of light.

To move into a full and complete conversation about your Unseen Self, you can then ask your trusted person, "If you had to pick a trait I'm unaware of, what would it be?" Or, "What have you noticed about what I do that's automatic?"

Once you get a few new learns, you can begin to understand more about your Unseen Self. Taking into account all the feedback you receive, you may see patterns—more than one person may have told you something similar.

These patterns carry more weight, and if more than one person sees a similar trait, than it could be true no matter how hard it is to face.

For now, tally up everything and consider your next actions. These could be to ease off a particular behavior that is damaging, or recognize it every time you do it. Then our Unseen Self is coming to the surface more each day, giving you an inside view of what you do and how it effects your happiness.

Ultimately, it is up to you to choose what is related to your happiness or not, and find some peace of mind in this process. This is the journey to your true self, not the destination. Take the feedback in, but don't let what you hear derail you. Keep moving forward and you'll be happy you did.

To recap the complete view of the self, here they are again:

1. The Me Self—known to all
2. The Secret Self—known to us but no one else
3. The Invisible Self—unknown to all
4. The Unseen Self—unknown to you but known to everyone else

These parts make up the big picture. If you add all these together, and everything you've learned, you can start to see a complete view of who you really are.

In its totality, the self is everything we like and don't like. If you choose to recognize it all, you will find the core of your personal sense of happiness.

CHAPTER FIVE

Getting to know ourselves is often a bumpy road. That's because we get to see ourselves for everything we are even if at first that might be difficult to stomach. Though the way we're about to do it will be like a walk in the park, comparatively.

It's small actions which, in the end, add up to create our total sense of who we are. It may seem comprehensive to consolidate everything we've taken note of, but it will give us a solid sense of our happiness and self. To start off, we'll create our "I Am" list.

It's exactly what the title implies as a catalogue that represents everything you've uncovered up to this point. To the best of your ability, you will take note of everything about who you think you are.

Each statement in your I Am list, both good and bad, will start with "I am," and be followed by the new perception or affirmation gained in the previous chapter.

These items could be activities, roles, careers, hobbies, bad habits, personality traits and/or negative declarations—anything you deem to be a true representation of yourself.

Examples of what it could include: I am a mac and cheese guru, I am a mother, I am a father, I am often indifferent, I am a smoker, I am not enough, or I am ambitious. The goal of this task is not to write what you wish you were, but who you really are. Including your fears, doubts and negative perceptions.

We've made some space for your new self to write so you can quickly jot down your I Am list. Try not to get hung up on any one of the affirmations, and move through the activity with little judgment or hesitation. Express yourself totally in the next couple of pages and don't worry about how you may come off. Just be honest. Be real.

You don't have to stop with the pages given. There may not be enough space to write everything you've learned or connections you've made.

In that case, grab an extra piece of paper or one of your devices and continue writing until you feel you have represented yourself completely.

Remember, this is not a competition of who has the most on their list. Your final self-inventory could have ten or one hundred things. It's totally up to you. If you'd rather skip the writing and just make a mental note of your new learns, then do so.

When you're ready, find a quiet space and summarize the notes from the four parts of yourself. Here's a refresher:

1. The Me Self—known to all
2. The Secret Self—known to us but no one else
3. The Invisible Self—unknown to all
4. The Unseen Self—unknown to you but known to everyone else

You can dedicate a quarter of your list to each, seeing how each self may represent different aspects of you. You can now fire away on your I Am list:

I am

_____

I am

_____

I am

_____

I am

_____

I am

_____

I am

_____

I am

_____

I am

_____

I am

_____

I am

_____

I am

_____

I am

_____

I am

_____

I am

_____

I am

_____

I am

_____

I am

_____

I am

_____

I am

_____

I am

_____

I am

_____

I am

_____

Right now, your list may seem like a bunch of random and unorganized thoughts. Plus, it may seem like you just got done beating yourself up.

So take it easy and know that the main chunk of the work is done. Now the enjoyable part begins—making sense of it all.

Primarily, we have to review our overall identity and the way we see ourselves. To do this, we will divide and conquer and split up the negative and positive statements. We will put a plus sign (+) next to the positive statements and minus sign (-) next to the negative ones.

Remember, this is an individual process. In the example I Am list, the statement "I am ambitious," to me, is a positive quality. So I would put a plus sign next to it. However, you might feel it is a negative trait and put a minus instead.

You may be tempted to get help from your friends, but don't. It's completely up to you what is considered a positive or negative characteristic. This list is an "I Am" proclamation, not a "What they think about me," list.

Others might influence us to change or add to our list and that would defeat the whole purpose of this exercise. It's all about you for a change, so enjoy this "me time."

An example of what your list could look like is:

> I am a mac and cheese guru +
> I am a father +
> I am often detached -

When you're finished, count up the pluses/minuses and then put that number below.

Positive: _____   Negative: _____

You can compare the positives against the negatives. This will help you get a complete sense of the "temperature" of your true self—what it is now—allowing you to see the whole picture, not just the individual parts.

If you have more pluses than minuses, then most likely you have a more positive self-view. If you have more minuses, then you might have a slightly more negative self-image. And if your marks are equally distributed, then you might have a more balanced outlook.

This list is not a strict indicator of your permanent view of yourself. Instead, it's how you presently see yourself and how you will eventually move toward a happier existence. If you're at all dissatisfied with the results, you can amend them.

Your next mission is to add new positive actions that, if nurtured, will become reality.

Find each negative statement (minus sign) and next to it write an affirmation, hobby, role or activity that you would like to see yourself doing more of or a positive trait you know to be true.

The statements do not have to be related to the negative idea, but do need to be two things: first, they have to be completely new, and second, they have to be doable.

You must have the ability to achieve the new affirmation. If one of your negative affirmations was, "I am very dependent on others." A possibly impossible positive statement would be, "I will live on my own starting tomorrow!"

Although this might be what you want in the future, it might not be obtainable all at once or now. A better positive vow would be, "I will try a new independent activity, like walking around the block alone, by the end of this week."

It's about seeing ourselves in a different light and not necessarily changing anything. We're going to allow the negatives to stay, but also encourage ourselves to see a better future.

An example of this is:

> <u>I am a mac and cheese guru +</u>
> <u>I am a father +</u>
> <u>I am often detached –</u> *I am a*
> *homework helper*

Next to "I am detached," it is not written, "I will become extra engaged," which may be a future desire. Instead, it is an achievable and healthy activity—"I am a homework helper."

No doubt, in the past, you have thought about how you wished you could adjust your negative perceptions and traits. But have you ever documented exactly how you would do that?

Growth is only possible when you're ready and want it to happen. You could spend all day adding affirmations to your list and then feel like you're hitting your head against a wall if your ideas are outside your reach.

If you add new and accomplishable statements, then you're not forcing a change. Instead, you can naturally growing toward being a fully realized and happier person.

When we examine everything—the bad and the good—and then we give ourselves progressive encouragements, we can feel a sense of wholeness. By acknowledging everything, we're laying a solid foundation for the rest of our journey.

Take your time adding actions since they will help you create a happier future. You can flip back a couple of pages and finish up when you can.

When you're ready to come back, we'll give this the fuel it deserves. We'll discover how our thoughts could be running our happiness show.

***

We think a lot. On average, we have between 25,000 and 50,000 thoughts a day.[1] What's happening upstairs can affect our feelings, moods, and sense of self.

We will notice much of our awareness sprang from internal sensations, and by asking others for their feedback and then writing down what we believed to be true representations, we were using our thought patterns to help us sift through what was fact and fiction.

Our thoughts played a crucial role in helping us uncover our true identity. Our natural thought patterns—whatever those may be—are related to who we are.

René Descartes famously asserted, "I think, therefore I am." Referencing how our thoughts are inexplicably linked to our identities, Buddha proclaimed, "We are what we think. All that we are arises with our thoughts."

Our thoughts are similar to a get-together with your friends. If we walked into the room with a blind fold covering our eyes, we'd get a lot of noise. Yet from that clamor, we would know what kind of event it was—a college party, an after work happy hour or just a couple of friends with a bottle of wine.

When we acknowledge our thoughts, the overall or average condition of our thoughts—positive or negative—we uncover a pattern. This is like fastening a microphone to the inside of our mind. What we get back can be jumbled and quickly move from one thought to the next but eventually reveals more about who we really are.

When we focus on certain thoughts, like striking up a conversation, we can understand how they affect our self-perceptions and our happiness. From there, we can tease out specific thoughts which may be hindering us from living a better life or some that will catapult us closer to discovering our personal satisfaction.

This is not to say that all negative thoughts are bad and all good thoughts will bring us happiness. A little bit of disparaging babble is actually a good thing because it pushes us to grow and an occasional cautious internal voice is better than an ungrounded optimistic one.

So ups and downs are natural. It would be nearly impossible to eradicate all negative thoughts, nor would we want to do this. Because happiness is not outside our reach, our negative thought pattern might be a part of that progression and it's our end goal to listen and understand.

We may have taken actions in the past to wrangle the internal chatter because, let's face it, our thoughts can sometimes get out of hand. They can sometimes keep us up at night, making us feel down and making everyday stressors seem like monstrous obstacles.

Many of us have negative thoughts—about ourselves, others, our situations and so on. Yet some may have more negative static than others, often making them feel almost powerless to stop the internal rant. It's like someone else is driving their car dangerously close to the edge of a cliff.

The most common recommendation is to repress negative thoughts, to tuck them away until they change their tune. From there, you're supposed to try your best to not to think those things or "release" the thoughts. Merely making them disappear and dissolve.

Some of us might have tried to write down our lousy thoughts throughout our day. An example could be, "I'm feeling miserable about my job," or "Why are my pants no longer fitting when yesterday they did?"

Trying to stop even one thought is the same as trying to stop a busted damn. It's almost impossible. That's because the more we put effort to prevent our internal chatter the louder it can get. Usually, what we focus on can become an exaggerated pain point. It can cause more harm than good.

Obviously, the approach of either releasing negative thoughts or writing them down has left many frustrated. The application of trying to stop a pattern is a significant undertaking. The alternative, though, of allowing your negative sensations to run the show is not always a lasting option.

It may seem obvious what persistently negative thoughts can do to our self-worth, identity and happiness over time, yet it might be surprising to learn how habitual and unnoticeable they have become.

For example, consider the statement, "I would like to go back to school." This is a noble goal, but one that is all too often followed by thoughts like these:

> "I don't have the time."
> "I don't have enough money."
> "I'm not smart enough."
> "I couldn't do all the work required."

We may have become accustomed to talking ourselves out of things. Our thoughts, whatever they may be, from "I hate my clothes" to "I'm not good enough," can become a pattern that we're often oblivious to, affecting our perceptions of ourselves and happiness.

One of the best techniques that has been proven to build a healthier self-image, thoughts and happiness is *self-talk*.

Today's self-talk reinforces the thoughts and ideas that can propel us closer to knowing our personal happiness and self-worth. It's investing in personal growth, instead of pumping ourselves up to achieve a goal.

Utilizing self-talk in our daily routine can help us emphasize the thoughts that make us better-off. Such reinforcements can help us discover greater happiness and generate new opportunities.[2]

To truly advance our overall thoughts, we will invest in the patterns that will eventually and positively impact our happiness. It's not about stopping any thought, or even changing your thoughts. It's about overriding the negative cycle.

You do not have to become a more positive thinker to be a happier person. Rather, you will take survey of the landscape of your mind and then reinforce the thoughts that will help you uncover your happiness.

To become aware of this pattern and the individual thoughts that form it, you will consider an idea or a project you recently wanted to start.

It could be learning to skate, building a dog house, having a dinner party, getting a softball team started at work, starting a business or even cooking a soufflé. The only thing it has to be is something that, if accomplished, would make you feel positive about yourself. Now think about what you'd like to start and begin to focus on it.

When you focus on this single thought, what happens?

The sensations pulsing through you should feel good because you're considering a positive and new venture. Now, expand your thoughts a little further outside your happy bubble. What are your thoughts saying about this idea?

By opening your awareness up to all your thoughts, you are allowing your basic pattern to surface. It is similar to the way you would uncover other portions of your life. You could see the bigger picture if you considered how everything fit together.

If thoughts are left isolated, then it is difficult to see the overall reasons. When you expand that singular moment into an entire imprint, it becomes a complete picture.

Think about when you recap your day to a friend. If you were to say, "They took away my lunch." It wouldn't make much sense. But if you instead said, "The salad was expired, and then they took away my lunch." There is a broader awareness to the narrative.

In group projects, this is often called a "think tank" in which everyone throws out every possible thought they have about a new idea. You can do the same with any thought or idea you may have.

It's like taking a pulse check and acknowledging the thoughts which may be stopping you from experiencing a more fulfilling life and, vice versa, the concepts that could fast track you closer.

The connections you make from one thought to the next forms a web. The interlocking of ideas is what creates your overall pattern. You'll see how each new thought can have many latent thoughts surrounding it. If you can get to the bottom of your thought chamber (the jumble of thoughts that create your overall viewpoint) and do not like what you find, that's okay.

Your pattern is not a strict indicator of your complete view. If you're unhappy with what bubbles to the surface with this simple exercise of choosing one thought and seeing where it leads you, you can rework it. You can invest in the ideas that you believe will get you closer to the life you were meant to live.

The first action you'll take is investing in an overall better thought pattern. Basically, you'll reinforce the personal chatter that can help you grow your personal happiness and sense of self.

Imagine your idea again and the thoughts tied to it. Now, one by one, you'll invest in the ones that will help you become happier.

To help you see where one thought can take you, you can use this next example as fuel for your first action. Let's say I wanted to start a business. Immediately, my mind goes in four directions:

1. Get a DBA
2. Get a website
3. Get a tax ID
4. Get a lawyer.

Each idea has thoughts associated with it. If I were to strike up a conversation with the notion of "getting a lawyer," my mind might turn to "What if I fail?" Or "What if I get into a legal battle?"

These thoughts can kick up anxious feelings. If I were to practice investing in healthier views, I would then apply this consideration, "I would have a lawyer if something were to go wrong."

I didn't stop the thoughts from rushing in or change the course of where they were headed. Instead, I invested in a perception that would ultimately make me happier when accomplished.

If you do the same, you can start to feel a bigger sense of lasting satisfaction. It's like investing your money. You wouldn't sink your money into a bad investment that wouldn't yield positive returns. So why would you invest in thoughts that will not encourage you to take positive actions?

You don't have to think good thoughts to make this work. In fact, you could have disparaging internal rants. The idea is not what caused you to stay unhappy or continued your lousy cycle; it's how you reinforce the thought that gives it power.

In the earlier example about starting my business, I could have let my doubt about "What if something bad happens?" Derail my entire desire and ultimate fruition of my goal. Instead, I can create a different perspective and turn anything around on a dime.

You can and will do the same once this becomes part of your everyday routine. Instead of thoughts being habitual and automatic, you will have beamed a spotlight on them and can see them for what they are; a fluctuating expression of your mind trying to make sense of the internal and external experience you have created.

Again, consider your idea, but this time think about all the positive actions you could take starting today to make this happen. It could be a new practice, a positive affirmation from earlier, or decide that each investment you make toward a thought will grow.

Then take a few minutes each day to think of this new venture and place positive and actionable thoughts behind it. If bad thoughts rush in, you can replace them with something you know to be fact and something you can accomplish without changing anything about yourself or life.

By generating and investing in the thoughts which can bring us joy, we are illustrating how our invested thoughts have more value than the discouraging ones.

Once we learn how to do this, no thought, no matter how critical, will stop us from finding our happiness. It's not about the thoughts you have. It's about how you allow them to advance your contentment.

It's like making a clearing for your happiness. It can't grow unless you cut back some over grown obstacles. In doing so, you are creating a healthier thought pattern and cycle.

Both actions, the I Am list and investing in compelling thoughts, allow us to examine our true-self in a logical and organized way.

If your disparaging thoughts get out of control in the future, you can come back to these practices. If you discover a new facet to your self-view, our I Am list can grow, too.

Both applications are at your disposal, making the process of knowing ourselves more enjoyable.

Our natural thought pattern and inner self have been uncovered. Though, it cannot be over-stressed, learning about yourself is a lifelong process. Negative thoughts come and go. Luckily, what makes you truly happy is often more consistent. Now, you will know, without a doubt, what makes you happy.

PART 1
KNOW WHAT MAKES YOU HAPPY

CHAPTER SIX

What makes us truly happy is somewhat consistent and deeply rooted in our *intrinsic motivators*. These "drivers" propel us into the life we've always wanted to live and, if allowed to expand, can multiply. In fact, our happiness is more directly related to internal influences rather than external factors.

In 1940, Harry F. Harlow first popularized the concept of intrinsic motivators when he set out to prove that motivation was both measurable and rule-based. He did this by studying monkeys and gave each a wooden game that had latches and pins (similar to a puzzle).[1]

The expectation was that the monkeys would only complete the toy if given an external motivator, such as a treat.

Shocking Harlow and others, the monkeys completed the activity of their own volition. No external motivation was necessary, and this stumped Harlow.

If it wasn't an external reason that compelled the monkeys to do the task, then what was it?

Harlow concluded it must be an internal trigger, "a third drive," called our "intrinsic motivation."[2] This drive is not excited by reward or lack of reward, but instead it's engaged when we do something that is challenging *and* enjoyable. Because the monkeys liked the game and the skill it took to complete it, they played without incentive.

This prompted more experiments, including one by Edward Deci in 1964 which demonstrated how money, as an external influence, can often lessen our intrinsic motivation to finish or even engage in a task or project.[3]

Another, more recent study, part of the *Journal of Happiness Studies*, discovered similarly that these kinds of activities which excite our intrinsic motivators by presenting challenge and excitement can generate a significantly higher level of happiness.[4]

An example is a person who enjoys snowboarding, and after shredding the slopes, enjoys a delicious dinner. Although both are enjoyed equally, snowboarding makes the person happier because it engages their intrinsic motivation. It's challenging and enjoyable which encourages their internal responses to engage.

The more we acknowledge and do things that are both pleasurable and difficult, the happier we can become. Activities like this are building blocks to our joy.

Granted, snowboarding might not be your cup of tea, but there are certain activities, tasks, roles, projects and occupations that engage your internal motivators, helping you feel a greater sense of contentment. Once you know what these activities are, you will uncover your natural *happiness triggers*.

Happiness triggers are our internal "switches" that are "turned on" when we engage with our core drivers. These are like thumb prints, no two triggers will be exactly the same. One person may find true elation in knitting a scarf while another might find the same sense surfing a twenty-foot wave.

Luckily, this works in our favor. If we all had the same motivators, we might face more competition in moving toward our ideal life. Varying triggers equate to an enormous diversity that can benefit all of us.

You might be thinking with less people fighting for a piece of happiness that it would mean a clearer path. However, it shouldn't be overlooked that once we know what makes us happy, we then have to do something about it.

The best way to work through busting your unhappiness cycle is to know what makes you naturally happier.

What is meant to surface is more knowledge of exactly the things that make you happy, so you don't have to chase after the things that won't bring you satisfaction and come back empty handed.

We're going to work from the inside out which will yield measurable and lasting results. We will uncover your happiness triggers and learn how to work with them, not against them.

If living a quiet and calm life is something you desire, then you can have it. Or if hightailing around the world on a cargo ship as a volunteer makes your heart sing, then you should have it, too. No matter what gets you out of bed in the morning, you will know it without a doubt.

CHAPTER SEVEN

-

Let's first consider a conundrum: often, we don't know what makes us happy until we see it, feel it or are faced with it.

Sometimes seeing is believing especially when it comes to your life satisfaction. To fully understand your *intrinsic motivators*, you will work through the "Let's Be Happy" practice.

It will represent the activities, jobs, roles, sports, or projects that are challenging yet enjoyable to you. Within this activity, you will find two separate sections. One is "Take the Happiness Challenge" and the other is "Take a Load Off. Enjoy."

Under "Take the Happiness Challenge," you will write all the activities that are challenging. Even if the task may seem small, you will still write it down.

These activities do not necessarily have to be enjoyable or negative, but they do have to take some amount of effort and often demand energy and concentration. For instance, we can love what we do for a living, but it can still be demanding.

This is a personal project and it is up to you to decide what is difficult. Take your time and choose activities that are both positive and negative.

In the "Take a Load Off. Enjoy," you will write all the activities that are enjoyable. Even if it is a small pleasure, you will add it. The activity you make note of must make you smile. These can be things like walking your dog, smelling fresh cut flowers, eating ice cream with your grandchildren, or spending time with your loved ones. There are many things that can bring us joy if we let them.

Think outside the box and choose activities and hobbies that give you a spark of creativity. Consider your passions and the inspirations that have not been fully expressed. The activities, jobs, and experiences you would like to have more often can be what you add to your page.

It would be similar to someone giving you the power to wish for a happier life. You then get to choose exactly what that experience should be.

This is your opportunity to see yourself in a new light. To create a possible reality where you get out of the same-old-stuff cycle and dropped into the life you have always envisioned for yourself. Instead of feeling like you're turning a massive ship against the wind, you can pivot slightly and go in the direction you want.

If we can foresee the things that will make us naturally happier, we can put self-doubt or worry behind us because we have a goal that represents our natural drives. Once you can see the finish line, no matter how far away it is, you can cross it.

No more swimming upstream. When life, people, or situations get you down, you can remember you have powerful internal motivators that are as unique as you are.

You were born with these motivators and they might have been hidden for most of your life. Now you will merely recognize them and then activate them.

This will carry through the rest of your movement toward living a more fulfilling experience, so relax and play around with many activities. Here's a quick example, check out this hypothetical father's Let's Be Happy page:

Take the Happiness Challenge
    -Career demands
    -Keeping up with everyone's schedules
    -Being a good dad

Take a Load Off. Enjoy.
    -Yoga
    -Watching movies
    -Playing with my kids

Now, it's your turn to catalogue your challenges and pleasures on your Let's Be Happy page:

Take the Happiness Challenge

_____

_____

_____

_____

_____

_____

<u>Take a Load Off. Enjoy.</u>

It might have taken a little effort to get started, but then it should have flowed. Your page represents everyday activities which are both enjoyable and difficult.

Separately, they embody isolated drives, but together they will uncover your *happiness triggers* (intrinsic motivators) and your new definition of personal happiness.

The relationship between the enjoyable aspects of your life and the taxing ones will reveal your baseline happiness. Up to this point, it could have felt, your happiness was behind a veil which made it difficult to see clearly. Now you can remove that thick layer and see the positive connections in your experiences.

By asking for advice or opinions, you're possibly defeating

the whole purpose of finding your own happiness triggers. So take your time to make the connections on your own.

In your Let's Be Happy page, you will put a happy face or a simple mark next to the connections between your delightful activities and the difficult tasks.

Here's an example, check out the hypothetical father's Let's Be Happy page again with the additions:

Take the Happiness Challenge
    -Career demands
    -Keeping up with everyone's schedules
    -Being a good dad ☺

Take a Load Off. Enjoy.
    -Yoga
    -Watching movies
    -Playing with my kids ☺

Now revisit your Let's Be Happy page and make the necessary mark-ups by adding your own variation of the happy face next to the ones that are related.

After you have marked up your page, you can choose your top three triggers which will have two characteristics. First, they give you a sense of purpose and, second, they energize you.

We'll define "purpose" as an activity, skill, or career that gives you a sense of centeredness. It is your intention or objective in life.

Simply, if you didn't do the things that bring you a sense of purpose, you wouldn't be you. It could be anything—surfing, horseback riding, being a good employee, being the best parent you can, being in service of others, being a firefighter, being a police officer, serving your country, or being an awarded chef. Whatever defines your true self and gives you a sense of belonging, big or small, is a top happiness trigger.

From there, your top motivators have to excite you. These

are your passions and the activities that cause strong sensations of motivation. They make you instantly happier when you engage in them and you want to be consistently immersed in them.

Again, in the hypothetical dad's example, "being a good parent" was what he felt was his purpose and "playing with his kids" is truly enjoyable.

Overall, his top happy trigger would be *being a phenomenal parent*. It makes him the happiest and gives him drive. Your top triggers will have these two qualities: purpose and enrichment.

By jotting down your motivators and combining your challenges and enjoyments into one statement, you are clearly defining and acknowledging your individual happiness. If asked in an elevator what makes you happy, you should be able give an answer in a flash. It demonstrates that your well-being is central to your life.

Next, select your top three happiness triggers with this in mind: they will tag along for the rest of the book.

My Top 3 Happiness Triggers:

_____

_____

_____

Congrats! Go ahead, we'll wait for your mini-celebration. Your main goal was to know what makes you happy, and guess what? You now do.

Your top three happiness triggers represent your main drivers in life. They influence "how" you will break of your unhappiness cycle.

No matter what happens to you throughout your experiences, you can fall back on these as your unalienable truths. Now your only responsibility is to move on to the next methodology to plot the course you'll take to end up in your final happy destination.

PART II

TELL OTHERS WHAT MAKES YOU

CHAPTER EIGHT

There is something to be said for those who know what they want and can easily voice it.

Think about a time when you told to a friend, "I *want* a new job." Then your friend connected you with someone who was hiring for an ideal position. It happened because you knew what you wanted and then opened up.

Knowing what you want is a third of the battle. You then have to take action, and the natural progression is to tell someone what you have decided.

We are communicating machines, and when we say our desires to others, we have a genuine opportunity to make them into an everyday experience.

In fact, the more we talk about something, the more it becomes possible for us to make it a reality.[1] Once it is said, your happiness becomes a truth or fact in your life. It has the power to become real.

When you talk about your happiness triggers, your closest friends and family can help you get to your final destination faster. It will open up doors you never thought were possible.

Though not all of us are talkative and may feel awkward opening up to such a degree, it's important for our happiness journey. When we express our happiness, we're giving it a place to grow and clearing a path for us to move down. Essentially, by expressing ourselves, we're demonstrating we take our happiness seriously and take responsibility for the outcomes.

Communicating helps us define our identity, form relationships and refine our happiness. By interacting with others, we can form and foster better connections with like-minded people and expand our compassion and empathy.

Think about having an exercise buddy—someone who will wake you up at the crack of dawn, make sure you're sticking to your lean meals and working out with you until you both feel the burn. Their job is considerable in your journey toward a healthier lifestyle because there is a certain level of accountability. You are accountable for facilitating their healthier lifestyle and they're responsible for you, too.

Telling others what makes you happy is a similar concept. Once you express your personal happiness, the other person becomes an accountability partner—a happiness buddy—and they can ask you how you are progressing, what actions you've taken and observe if you slip up through your journey.

This works in your favor. Once you open up to others, you can create a supportive network that genuinely wants to see you thrive.

To start, we have to get talking. This also means we have to get social. Our sense of happiness is reinforced and influenced by face-to-face interactions.[2] In fact, being social is one of the greatest predictors of personal satisfaction.[3]

Happiness is then a social experience and an "emotional contagion."[4] It rapidly "spreads" from one person to the next.[5]

Your happiness is related to your friends' happiness, their friends' happiness and then their friends' friends' happiness.[6] It's not only your friends' happiness rubbing off on you, but your happiness influencing them, too. Everyone benefits from happy people.

For example, if you have a positive friend, their mood will rub off on you, eventually making you happier. Then, your happiness rubs off on them and your other friends, continuing to swirl positivity which will eventually affect everyone around you.

In fact, each happy person we socialize with can increase our own happiness by as much as 25%. By comparison, a raise at work can only, on average, increase our happiness by 2%.[7] Being social with happy people is then similar to getting almost twelve monetary raises, instantly.

It may seem, then, that the more people we know and are social with, the better-off we can become. However, just because we have lots of friends doesn't mean we'll necessarily be happier.

Instead, you will focus on the closest people in your life that can help you become more prosperous. Our level of happiness is directly related to our intimate relationships, close friends, and shared interest groups, meaning we shouldn't need to go far to find the people who will make us the happiest.

The Top 3 Predictors To Your Happiness:

1. Socializing with people who have similar interests and beliefs
2. Maintaining close friends and relationships
3. Meeting and seeing them regularly

You may be wracking your brain trying to figure out what groups or activities have all three predictors for happiness. To researchers, a good place to start was church.

Chaeyoon Lim and Robert Putnam found that churchgoers reported their friendships at church made them happier than other relationships because of shared interests and beliefs.[8] With regular meet-ups, that were reinforced on a weekly basis, Lim and Putnam concluded that these characteristics tended to create closer friendships.[9]

Any regular meeting, religious or not, which reinforces

close relationships can increase happiness and your quality of life. In fact, the diversity of our social connections significantly influences our life satisfaction.[10]

One example is volunteering. Volunteering increases the three predictors to happiness. People who volunteer report a greater sense of joy than those who don't, because it encourages empathic emotions—feelings associated with happiness—and supports shared interests, making and maintaining close friendships and regular meetings which all add up to a positive outlook.[11]

Socializing doesn't require you to become someone you're not. It's interacting with people who are both similar and dissimilar to you, and then engaging with both your close friends and with people who can, over time, change your perceptions in a positive way.

You already know who your close friends are, but you may not have realized how each reinforces and influences your happiness.

Think back to Part I about "The Unseen Self." We asked our closest relationships what kind of person we might be. The people you chose can now be your happiness buddies and eventually, you'll be telling your happiness to them. They are critical to giving your happiness a clear voice.

To appreciate this more fully, we will consider and identify our best relationships based on intimacy, similar interests and regular meet-ups.

We might find it easier to look at our current connections with a bird's eye view, seeing our interactions as interlocking because they're not always separated into ideal categories. For instance, your sister might be a family member and your best friend.

You can consider your top connections based on the type of relationship you share with each:

1. Close relationships—example: family, your significant other and/or close friendships

2. Similar interests—example: social media friends and/or interest groups

3. Regular meet-ups—example: work friends, sport teams and/or friends who are close in proximity

The people who you're thinking of which fall into these three categories are the first you will tell your happiness to. That's because you trust them and they are part of your happiness network. Now all you need to do is *tell* them your happiness to create a more blissful experience.

CHAPTER NINE

There aren't many things we like talking about more than our own happiness. In fact, our brains seem to be wired to enjoy not only expressing it, but also listening to other people's as well.[1]

Your close connections are your primary touchstones throughout this process because they're, hopefully, supportive in your journey.

By sharing, you're reinforcing your happiness, making valuable connections, becoming a better communicator and ultimately refining what makes you happy. It's like adding the final polish. This will make your best life more obtainable and easily expressible to the rest of your network.

Think about a recent and important conversation you had with someone close. Then, consider how you told them your thoughts.

Most likely, you explained them step-by-step, then the benefits and lastly, what you predicted the future results would be. Afterward, they may have had a chance to refine your idea to make it work in the real world.

Telling your happiness is similar to the way you naturally express yourself and can be broken down into four parts:

1. Telling it all
2. What benefits me, benefits you
3. What my future life could be
4. What do you think?

1. Telling it all

This is your time to shine to your closest friends. You get to tell them everything you have learned thus far and express your happiness. Yet, before we dive into spilling the beans, we should take a moment to have a quick refresher.

Most likely, you regularly talk to your friends about what's on your mind. Now, you'll be adding a little extra style to what you say with "I believe" statements.

Back on your "I Am" list, you listed all the things you considered important to your identity and started each sentence with "I am..."

"I believe" statements are similar, except we will be starting our sentences with "I believe..." or "I feel ..." When you use "I believe" statements, you are making declarative statements that help you take charge of your communication, situations and ultimately, life.

Your happiness is important and it should be given the respect it deserves, simply shown through powerfully expressing yourself with these types of declarations.

When you're ready to express your satisfaction, you'll state, "I feel that (insert happiness here) makes me happy." Or, "I believe if I did more (insert happiness here) in my life, I'd be happier." Or, "I get excited about the possibility of (insert happiness here) being in my life more often."

For now, though, let's consider the next few actions before we use our new powerful, yet simple, communication technique.

2. What benefits me, benefits you

It would be selfish to keep your happiness to yourself after learning how contagious a positive outlook can be. Most of us need a pick-me-up every once in a while and when you're not feeling well, you're happy friends will be there. And vice versa, when they need you, your happiness can benefit them.

The benefits of happiness are vast and personal. One aspect that could improve from a sunnier disposition is your health. People who have a more positive outlook are less likely to get ill when exposed to illness than those who do not regularly engage in emotions associated with happiness (for instance: liveness and calmness).[1]

Also, your relationships will flourish. People want to be around happy people. It is infectious to be with someone who is grounded.

In the last chapter, we learned how a happy person could positively influence our lives with more positive feelings. Then their optimism will rub off on you and your friends.

The benefits of personal satisfaction can go beyond these. It can improve your cash flow, sleep, time management, your family, or the world. Expand your happiness bubble. What else can it improve or update if given a real chance to grow?

It does not have to be tangible; it can be conceptual. If you become a happier individual then you could feel more respected, the little "ant-bites" of the world wouldn't affect you as much. Or when you do "feel down," you can pull yourself up again and faster.

What you determine to be an outcome of being happier is up to you. For now, keep them close—we'll employ the benefits as we continue.

3. What my future life could be

If you could look into a crystal ball and see your happy future, what would it be? Would it be you engaging your passion all day? Would it be you traveling the world with your family? Would it be you and your friends beginning a startup? Or would it be starting your new job?

Predicting your life after you're regularly engaging in your happiness regularly can be a way to see yourself and life in a new light. It's realistically placing importance on what you foresee in the near future. This is the precursor to the actions you will take to make your happiness into a reality.

Today, your happiness has a better opportunity of being a reality than ever before. With the next action of sharing it, you are putting a possible stamp on your future.

You do not have to "dream" about happiness anymore. You know it and can tell others about it. It's similar to putting an "X" on top of your happiness road map. Once you know where the "landmarks" are and how to get there, your final destination is more accessible.

No longer do you have to accept a bleak future. You can foresee yourself being a happier person because you are shifting your direction in life. When you share the benefits of your happiness with others, your future could be the way you had envisioned it would be.

4.   What do you think?

We may have spent most of our lives "hearing" people, but *actively listening* puts us on a whole different communicational level. Active listening is when we intently listen and then summarize or repeat what someone has said.

Over time, this can not only improve our communication skills, but our empathy, which is associated with happiness. Once we are able to summarize what someone has already said, we are making a connection with them and forging a path for our happiness to flourish.

When you "tell" your happiness and then ask for suggestions, you will use active listening to help you refine your ideas.

First, you will listen to what the other person has said (verbally) and what their body language is expressing (nonverbally). More often than not, we place a higher importance on what is not said, rather than what is actually voiced. Often we cannot control what our bodies are revealing and we give away our "true" feelings more often than not.

For example: we could tell a close friend our happiness, then ask for their feedback. They may have said, "Sounds good to me," but their dropped eyebrows, crossed arms, and harsh tone said otherwise.

We all know this stuff because we do it every day. We're constantly watching non-verbal cues to assess the real message being given.

We can then utilize our active listening and pick up on the subtle cues to respond, "So you think it's good, but you may have some concerns?" Simply asking, "Did I hear you right?" Or, "Is this what you meant?" Can improve our active listening skills and refinement of our happiness.

We don't want to get wires crossed. These people will be a part of busting our unhappiness cycle, so now is not the time to lose their support through miscommunication. Active listening will ensure you heard them loud and clear with their support in mind.

You are capturing what they've communicated and what they meant. Another example is if a friend said, "I like your happiness plan, but have you considered where you're going to get the money, time and people?"

The active listening summary could be, "Are you *worried* I haven't considered *resources, a timeline, and people?*"

Buzzwords not only show you were listening, but also demonstrates you take your friend's feedback and your happiness seriously.

By recapping what they've proposed in two to five key words, you have encouraged the possible refinement of your happiness.

Now you should feel like a communicational genius...or at least conversationally smarter. In fact, you will have graduated with flying colors once you complete the next action—proudly expressing your happiness.

By now, your happiness should be becoming second nature. You've lived with it for the last few chapters and should be able to talk about it effortlessly.

It can be easier to remember power statements that are short and to the point. To give you the same boost, we'll be formulating your happiness in the same way—brief and commanding.

Below, there is space for you to write, but you can also just think about how you would share your happiness:

I believe my happiness is

_____

_____

_____

It can benefit us because of

_____

and   _____

In the future, I see my happiness improving

_____

So, what do you think?

The only thing that could be standing in your way do doing this action is time. Life is busy and carving out time for ourselves is difficult enough, let alone meeting up with someone else.

To make this process easier, you can either set a date for expressing yourself or be spontaneous and when an opportunity arises, tell them your happiness.

We know how important this is not only for our self-growth but also for those around us. Remember, once you turn the page to telling your happiness, there's no turning back. Ultimately, we have the responsibility to make this into a reality.

It might be easy to put this feat on the back burner, but today, we can start talking. The possibilities of how you'll do it are endless, but here are a few ideas to get started:

1.   Party on happiness!

Not only is it a happy time for all, but you're also getting social, spreading happiness and conveying your motivations all at the same time. It's a happiness party where you get to express your joy and encourage others to do the same.

For this party, you don't need streamers, cake or pointed hats (unless you want them). Instead, you'll need a healthy helping of good friends, food and conversation.

Pick a time, date and place—it's better in a quiet space so everyone can listen and be heard. From there, get creative. Start with "I believe" statements, then the benefits, the future and lastly, open up the conversation with space for ideas.

Everyone can join in expressing their happiness and, yes, their cheerful edits.

Have fun and relax. The people you invite, your friends and family, should support you through this process and be included.

If your happiness is a positive force then your closest people can help make it into a reality. Take this opportunity to share what's in your heart. It should be received by those who love you and will give you the guidance you need.

2. Coffee with a heart-shaped pastry

Who doesn't have time for coffee? You can make time for

your closest friends, just like they have made time for you in the past. It doesn't have to take long; only ten to fifteen minutes.

For these power sessions, it's important to have what you'll say ready to go. Being able to quickly express your happiness and then ask for refinement will help everyone stay on track.

Practicing what you'll say and how you'll say it leaves more time for questions. Just like when you present at the office, leaving ample time for Q&A at the end.

Even though this is a short get-together, it doesn't have to feel rushed. Let the other person know the reason they are there is primarily because they are loved and secondly, to help you fully express your happiness and make it into a possible reality.

3. Calling a team happiness meeting

Possibly, when you were young, your parent(s) had *family meetings* with you and your siblings to talk. They were everyday huddles where you talked about school, issues or even vacations.

Your team happiness meeting is similar because you will bring your closest people together. This will be like the happiness party, but you'll be the center of attention and the main one talking.

Invite your closest friends, family members and/or significant other to a quiet place—preferably your apartment/home. Then share your happiness.

If at first there is silence (this could happen), encourage conversation by asking, "What do you think?" Or, "What advice do you have for me?"

After you have fully expressed yourself and received feedback, you will have had a successful get together. Smiles can be passed around as you relish in the fact that you've completely expressed your happiness.

Whichever you choose—party on happiness, coffee and a heart-shaped pastry or calling a team happiness meeting—let it represent your own happiness journey and true self.

If, through the knowing section, you learned you are happiest when you're quiet, then maybe a one-on-one will work best for you. If you learned you like to be social, then have a happiness party!

This is a personal process and if you feel ready to tell your happiness to a couple of people, then move on. But if you need more refinement and belief in your happiness, then go back and keep working through these pages until you're ready to talk.

At the very least, you should consider telling at least one person who is close to you. This reinforces your happiness and encourages you to make it a real experience.

It is entirely up to you who you tell, when you tell them and how you'll do it, but remember it's better to do it sooner rather than later. Because it's fresh in your mind, now would be the best time to set something up, so go ahead and text, call, email, direct message, smoke signal or something to get your closest people on board.

You can put this book down and spend time telling the people who love you as much as you love them what makes you happy. When you're ready, you will come back to this book and complete your final action in breaking your happiness addiction: *do* what makes you happy.

PART III
DO WHAT MAKES YOU HAPPY

CHAPTER TEN

You get to *do* what makes you happy and actively engage with your bliss on a consistent basis. When doing your happiness, it is not finite. Instead, it's moving toward a lifestyle (a practice) of regularly interacting with the people, situations, things, and activities that help you become a happier person.

What you gain from this last action is measurable—you can touch, see and feel the outcome of all your hard work and something that can positively affect your life.

If you have doubt in your ability to perform your happiness, just look back on all the incredible work you've completed so far.

Throughout this book, you have done a lot of small tweaking. Slowly, you uncovered your true self through gathering all the correct information, then made a decision about your identity. Then, you utilized that knowledge to uncover your happiness triggers—the kind of deep satisfaction that could break your unhappiness cycle. From there, you told your closest relationships what makes you happy.

It's important to notice this was all already available to us. We did not have to go beyond our current life to discover our personal happiness. Or chase a sense of joy to only be disappointed with the outcome.

Before we dive head first into finally doing what makes us happy, we should consider what needs to be set up to bring our happiness into the real world. If we don't have our basic needs met and the things that are necessary to build a happier life, then we might not be successful.

We don't have to look further than our everyday lives for proof that our satisfaction is tied to what we need.

Think about your cell phone. Many would claim they couldn't live without it and we all might agree. Now, imagine you've lost it. A somber thought, but that chest pounding and throat closing sensation when we think we've lost our phone is actually a misplaced need. Our devices represent more than an object—they represent our need for connection and resources.

If our needs are not being met, basic or complex, then we will be more focused on getting what we need, rather than engaging with our happiness.

Reviewing our requirements will help us not only respect our desires, but also assess which are available, and how to meet them before we get into the big swimming pool of happiness.

<u>The 4 Main Categories of Needs</u>:

1. Emotional
2. Tangible
3. Environmental
4. Connection

<u>1. Emotional</u>

It's time to get in touch with our feelings. When we follow our hearts, we could be surprised by the sensations that get kicked up along the way. Although it is exciting to go after what we want, it can still be a journey with some twists and turns.

For example, if your happiness is being close to your family, but you and your family have become estranged it could have some unforeseen emotional hurdles. Depending on the way your current experience is set up, you could uncover many unexpected feelings. We will work on foreseeing our current and future needs to make this transition as smooth as possible.

In the beginning of the book, Dr. Sharot explains that if people are able to clearly foresee their future, they are happiest. As a result of engaging in our happiness, we should be able to imagine our future and how we will respond to it.

The emotions you may experience are personal and based on your new practices. One feeling we might all be experiencing as we start to do our happiness is fear.

Taking the leap toward your true motivations meant you had to get to know yourself, tell others about what makes you happy and now engage with your happiness on a whole new level. This process can be daunting and sometimes overwhelming.

Remember we are not changing anything about our lives to do our happiness, only making small adjustments. This journey is full of new feelings that, if respected and acknowledged, can be the gasoline for your happiness engine.

2.   Tangible

Like with anything in our lives, we have to get the foundation prepared to successfully launch. These are the objects, spaces and things you'll need to make your happiness into a reality.

Not to be confused with buying a new car, boat or hover craft (even though that would be pretty cool), these are the materials that need to be in place to make your happiness an everyday experience.

For instance, if your happiness was to start a new business, the tangible objects you might need could be a business plan, location, employees and office supplies.

If you were going to experience abundance on a more consistent basis, what would need to be in place? How would you reorganize your life to make this happen? What would need to stay or go?

Consider the answers to these questions to reveal the material aspects to your happiness.

3.   Environmental

Humans do not live in an environmental vacuum. Every part of our lives has the ability to affect other experiences. For example, if our work environment is making us unhappy, then this could leak into our personal lives as well. Creating a lousy home life, too.

There are specific environments which better support our happiness. Think about your favorite places to be in; like a coffee shop, your room, home, the beach or mountains. These spaces are more than locations—they're environments that resonate with you and give you what you need.

It would be unrealistic, though, to think we could change all of our environments to better suit our happiness. Unfortunately, some settings will remain the same no matter how we update them.

Though the ones you can adjust should reflect your true self and happiness.

Let's say the color blue is calming for you and makes you feel a sense of joy. But when you look around, everything in your home is red...In this case, your environment is not reflecting what makes you feel good or the aspects that you need to be happy.

Consider the hypothetical parent: his home is his happy environment. It's where he and his family live, play and love. For him to make this environment better suited for his happiness, he could set up a playroom for his kids and reorganize the home to more accurately represent him and his passions. This environmentally supports his happiness which is being a good parent.

Our environmental needs are important for satisfying our personal happiness and should be in place before we do what makes us happy.

4.   Connection

You may pride yourself as being a lone wolf, but not anymore. As seen in Part II Tell Others What Makes You Happy, we connected with our closest friends to reinforce our happiness and will do the same to be able to do our happiness.

Our need for connection can often be deep and shouldn't be taken lightly. Again, the fastest way to get happier, instantly, is to get social. Connection is a necessity of life and contentment.

Your social connections are vast. From work friends, college buddies, interest groups, and social media connections, you can have a wide variety of bonds. Each relationship is a stepping stone to living a more meaningful life and should add "positivity" toward your experiences.

If you do not see the value in your current relationships, then this could be an indication you have many acquaintances, yet no one who is close or you might have shut yourself off to bonding with others.

It's important to have people in your life who love you for who you are. So take this moment to covet those people who want to see you grow. These connections are a healthy part of your life and you can work toward cultivating them.

The Recap of Your Needs:

Let's revisit the example of the hypothetical parent and look through what his needs might be:

> Emotional: Respect, empowerment, love
>
> Tangible: Toys for the children, building materials for the new playroom
>
> Environmental: Playroom and open space
>
> Connection: Supportive significant other, close friends, children

This next part is up to you to complete and highlights

what needs are most important to you. Take your time to make declarative statements about the four areas of your needs.

<u>Respect My Needs</u>

<u>Emotional Needs:</u>

    Happiness
☐ Respect
☐ Acceptance
☐ Love
☐ Passion
☐ Peace
☐ Trust
☐ Empowerment
☐

<u>Tangible Needs:</u>

☐ Building materials
☐ Activity supplies (surfboard, diving gear, hiking boots, etc.)
☐ A home
☐ A wardrobe to match your true self
☐ Office supplies
☐ Home décor/materials
☐ Business plan
☐ Car/bike/bus pass
☐ Warehouse or Office Space

Environmental Needs:

Now you'll find a circle with lines jetting out from it. In the middle, you'll write one to three of your top places (environments) that make you the happiest. Along the lines, you can note the feelings, sensations and environmental uniqueness of each. This can give you clues as to how to transform your current environments to better suit your happiness.

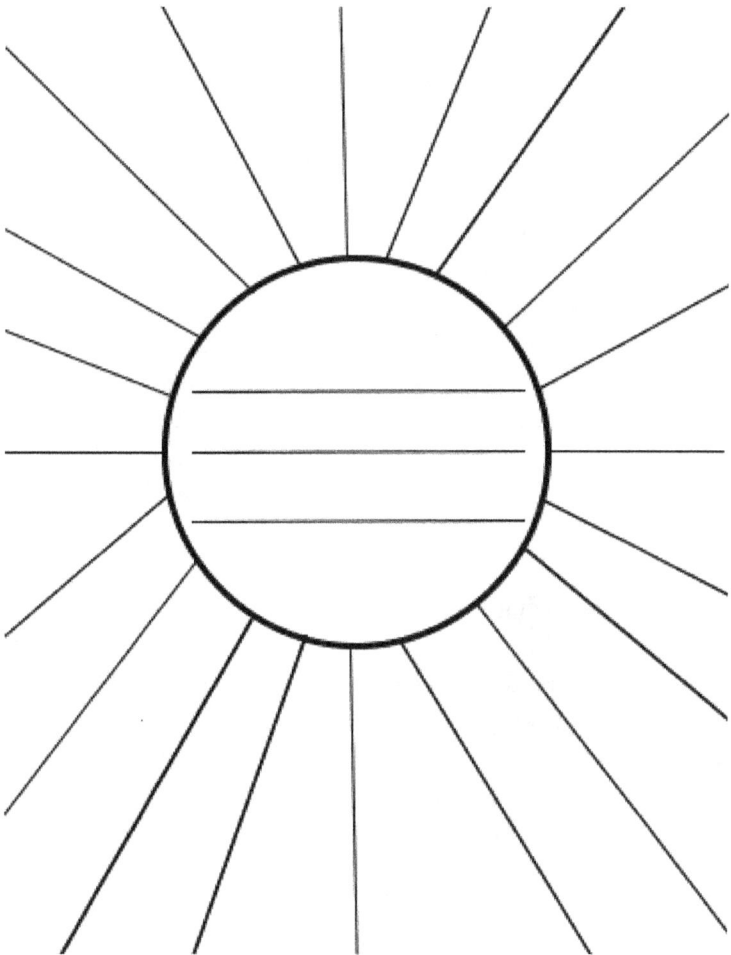

Connection Needs:

☐ Interest groups
☐ Shared activities
☐ Social media
☐ Close Friends
☐ Significant other
☐ Family

Admitting we have needs and recognizing which are being met, or not, can be the hardest part. By working through Respect My Needs, you might have quickly realized there are certain things that need to be set up to make everything come together.

Making small adjustments to better suit your necessities can make the biggest difference to your overall well-being. It makes doing your happiness easier. Once things are set up to your liking, you can engage with your satisfaction on a more consistent basis because it's readily available to you. It is within arm's reach.

By understanding our needs and the actions required to fulfill them, we are putting ourselves in the driver's seat and taking full responsibility for the outcome of our actions.

This process allowed us to assert our needs, possibly something we've never done before today. From now on, if we feel like our needs are not being met, then we'll know exactly which ones are being ignored and how that lack is affecting our happiness.

The time has officially come to get your needs met. This might take some time, so go out today and take action in gearing up your life and spaces to match your happiness.

When everything seems to be foundationally solid, you can come back to this book and dive into the best part—*doing* exactly what makes you happy.

CHAPTER ELEVEN

Now you're ready to take the final action: *do* what makes you happy. Your life and environments should already be set up to make accomplishing this last achievement fairly simple, so let's put the *action* in satis*faction*!

Doing your personal happiness is one of the most influential actions you will take, not just because it's the culmination of everything you've done thus far, but also because it gets you doing positive activities on a regular basis.

To do your happiness and make it lasting is simple. You'll spend a little extra time throughout your week—just five minutes to an hour a few times each week—on the activities that make you happier. Over time, these small actions can become a sustainable reality.

An example to get the gears rolling: let's say someone seriously enjoys watching television. In fact, as soon as they get home, they turn it on, but their top happiness trigger is cooking.

In that case, they can watch a cooking show a couple times a week, picking up a few free and fresh recipes. Then, they will *do* their happiness and cook a dish they've learned. Regularly cooking what they've learned is actively engaging with their happiness on a consistent basis and building a sustainable lifestyle focused on their well-being.

Take a deep breath. We can all do this. It does not require too much extra effort on our parts to get our lives pointed in the direction we want. Besides, we've come this far, so why not take the plunge? It is worth it.

To start, you'll choose activities surrounding your happiness that are ongoing, enhance your life and ultimately make you happier.

Ongoing

It's not just doing one big activity and then reaping the benefits of it later. Instead, it's engaging in regular activities that can cultivate well-being. Every day you will take time for your happiness and then do something that relates to it.

Your happiness is not a one-and-done deal. You have the incredible opportunity to do your happiness every day if you want to. Putting in the work today to engage in ongoing activities can make your personal happiness into lasting happiness.

You can accomplish and bring more of anything into your life if you take it one step at a time. If happiness is nurtured by ongoing action, it will thrive. And if the happiness you do is uniquely your own, it will last.

For example: if your happiness is being the best software engineer you can then every day you could learn a new platform or system, code, or take online courses to get more certifications. Sticking to something, then doing it consistently and finally completing it is bringing more positive outcomes into your life.

Enhance Your Life

Who doesn't want a little extra "good stuff" in their life? We could all benefit from extra time, money, love, health, opportunity and support starting today.

The activities you choose should enhance your life and place you in the power seat. You don't have to wait for someone to give you a big serving of happiness. You are the influencer, and by enhancing your experience, you are making it your own.

Everyone, including you, could use more of the things they want, so this is your chance to do activities that give you these enhancements.

For instance, if your happiness is surfing and you decide to teach surf lessons once a week, you will be enhancing your life by making more money and connections. By focusing on possible improvements, you are edging closer to doing your happiness on a more consistent basis.

Make You Happier

The outcome of doing these activities is often a more stable and fulfilling sense of joy. If you can commit yourself to regularly engaging in your happiness, then you can break your unhappiness cycle. You only have to dedicate some time to doing the things you like.

Once you pledge your time, the possibilities and positive outcomes are endless. The results from these activities are measurable. You can begin to feel your sense of happiness grow. Your stress will lower, and your relationships will flourish.

People will start to notice how things seem to fall into your lap and stay within your grasp for longer. Over time, this will encourage you to keep doing these activities on a more consistent basis.

Now that we've laid the ground rules for doing your happiness, your next big action is to complete your final expression of happiness: "I Do What Makes Me Happy."

Think about your top one to three happiness triggers from your "Let's Be Happy" page and begin considering the activities that surround each. These activities should be ongoing (sustainable), enhance your life (time, money, health, support, etc.), and make you happier when you get to do them more often.

Once you have your activities in mind, you're ready to

complete the last page. When you complete it, you can tear it out and pin it on your refrigerator, office cubical, frame it or take a picture of it on one of your devices and keep it close.

Your I Do What Makes Me Happy sheet should be within arm's reach most of the time to remind you that your happiness is an everyday and active practice.

<u>I Do What Makes Me Happy</u>

<u>Happy Trigger #1 (Intrinsic Motivator)</u>:

_____

_____

_____

Ongoing: How will you make this ongoing in your life?

_____

_____

_____

_____

_____

Enhancements:

- ☐ Money
- ☐ Love
- ☐ Time
- ☐ Support
- ☐ Relationships
- ☐ Health
- ☐ Career
- ☐ Family

Happiness Outcome:

Happy Trigger #2 (Intrinsic Motivator):

_____

_____

_____

Ongoing: How will you make this ongoing in your life?

_____

_____

_____

_____

_____

_____

Enhancements:

☐ Money
☐ Love
☐ Time
☐ Support
☐ Relationships
☐ Health
☐ Career
☐ Family

Happiness Outcome:

_____

_____

_____

_____

_____

_____

Happy Trigger #3 (Intrinsic Motivator):

_____

_____

_____

Ongoing: How will you make this ongoing in your life?

_____

_____

_____

_____

_____

_____

Enhancements:

- ☐ Money
- ☐ Love
- ☐ Time
- ☐ Support
- ☐ Relationships
- ☐ Health
- ☐ Career
- ☐ Family

Happiness Outcome:

_____

_____

_____

_____

_____

_____

You have just formulated your game plan! This is your blueprint for how you'll *do* what makes you happy.

Your activities are ongoing which means you can get started today. Plus, the enhancements not only give you validation toward your happiness, but also make your actions positive forces in your life. Lastly, the outcome is simple—you get to experience a spike in your happiness and bask in the rays of your satisfaction for longer periods of time.

Looking over your I Do What Makes Me Happy page, you'll notice that many of the activities include other people. Happiness is an interconnected and social experience, and will often involve more than just you which represents a holistic well-being.

This is an ongoing practice. Don't stop with what you've done thus far, because you might discover new ventures, activities or people who you want to add. You can come back to the resources in this book whenever you don't know, can't talk or are not sure what to do next.

Today Become a Happy Person:

In the know section, you defined yourself and your happiness. Through telling, you created a close happiness network that had your back every step of the way. Now you get to do what makes you happy on a consistent basis. The connection between knowing, telling and doing is inextricably linked and each builds upon the other.

The actions you take today are totally in your control and, if done consistently, could eventually take you where you want to go. The results are measurable. It is a happiness that's sustainable, can be seen and felt, and within your reach.

Everything is now on your side; you have ongoing activities which enhance your life and the outcome is your individual happiness. By taking measurable actions, we can get to where we want to go and, over time, stay there longer.

You are no longer pressured by the relentless hunt of happiness and have uncovered it within your current experience. It is not something you have to go out and get. You are on your way to breaking your unhappiness cycle.

This does not guarantee it will be easy at first or that you will notice a difference overnight. It could take some time to see noticeable results. We may have been living, behaving and feeling a certain way for a period of time so it could take a while to see everything come together, but it is well worth the effort and wait.

There is no such thing as a tiny act. Small and positive acts can add up to big and happy results.

Even if these acts seem insignificant in comparison to other actions throughout your day, they gradually build a more lasting and stable sense of happiness.

You can put this book down and do what makes you happier. You've just arrived at your happy destination. Your hard work has paid off. Your happiness is now *known, told and done.*

KNOWN, TOLD, DONE.

Through writing this book, a simple truth about happiness emerged. It can be addictive and difficult to find if not focused inward.

Happiness is a practice which produces all kinds of chemicals, and this "high" can cause us to tailspin into an unhappy cycle.

I believe if we can be happier individuals, the contagious nature of happiness, in theory, can make the world a happier place. It starts with us internally as individuals and then radiates outward.

Before this book, and the people that positively influenced my journey came into my life, I sustained a major setback which ironically became a springboard for one of the most extraordinary personal journeys.

A little over five years ago, I was hit with a truth about my self-identity—I was diagnosed with chronic depression. Life was a series of unfortunate events chained together that formed years of disappointment. I suffered from severe depression and felt like I had hit a wall. I turned to my doctor for help and she prescribed medication and recommended I see a professional.

Her diagnosis was that I would *always* suffer from depression based on my genetics and history. My outlook was bleak and sad.

But I wanted to give happiness one more try. Instead of going on the medication, I gave myself one year to get happy. If I couldn't do it on my own, I would apply more drastic measures and take my doctor's recommendations.

I knew it was a risky and dangerous decision. I had ongoing and systemic depression which seemed, more often than not, to flirt with my own demise. In my gut, though, I knew it was the right path—the path back to happiness.

From there, I read every major self-help book. I went to seminars all over the nation and changed everything about my life. I changed my job, moved across the country, changed my friends, relationships, clothes, and the list went on, but it didn't end happily ever after.

After one year, I revisited my original plan and felt like I had failed. I was *still* miserable.

The year of searching for more happiness through conventional and mass techniques left me empty handed. I was still just as depressed. I chased after happiness that was just outside my reach. I had unintentionally become addicted to the "happy high."

After my year of chasing happiness, my beliefs, outlooks, and life changed.

Now, I believe there is a better way to be happy. The people who have helped make this book into a reality have been with me every step of the way. These have mainly been my mom, dad, twin sister, younger sister, younger brother, my step brothers, grandparents, extended family and friends who never gave up on me or my desire to write this book.

I am endlessly grateful and happy to have a loving and supportive network of people in my life. Without them, I am not sure if I'd still be here today and expressing these messages. To find lasting happiness, you must know, tell and then do.

ENDNOTES

Chapter 1

1. American Society of Addiction Medicine. (2011). The latest definition of addiction. *Addiction Today*. Retrieved from http://www.addictiontoday.org/addictiontoday/2011/10/latest-definition-of-addiction.html.
2. Psychologies (2014, April. Boost your natural 'feelgood' chemicals. *Psychologies*. Retrieved from https://psychologies.co.uk/self/how-to-boost-your-natural-feelgood-chemicals.html
3. Healthline (2012). Unhappiness by the numbers: 2012 depression statistics. *Heathline*. Retrieved from http://www.healthline.com/health/depression/statistics-infographic.

Chapter 2

1. Santa Maria, C. (2012). Positive thinking: questioning its power. *Huffington Post*. Retrieved from http://www.huffingtonpost.com/2012/06/04/positive-thinking_n_1568684.html.

Chapter 3

1. Wellcome Trust (2011). Blame 'faulty' frontal lobe function for undying optimism in face of reality. *Science-Daily*. Retrieved from http://www.sciencedaily.com/releases/2011/10/111009140201.htm
2. Sharot, T., Korn, C. W., & Dolan, R. J. (2011). How unrealistic optimism is maintained in the face of reality. *Nature Neuroscience, 14*(11), 1475-1479
3. Sharot, T. (2012, December 31). The optimism bias. *The Guardian*. Retrieved from http://www.guardian.co.uk/science/2012/jan/01/tali-sharot-the-optimism-bias-extract
4. Sharot, T. (2012, February). The optimism bias [Video file]. Retrieved from http://www.ted.com/talks/tali_sharot_the_optimism_bias.html.
5. Minasian, J. (2012). Interview with Dr. Tali Sharot, (Neuroscientist). Retrieved from https://www.publishgoodink.com/press
6. Minasian, J. (2012). Interview with Dr. Tali Sharot, (Neuroscientist). Retrieved from https://www.publishgoodink.com/press
7. Minasian, J. (2012). Interview with Dr. Tali Sharot, (Neuroscientist). Retrieved from https://www.publishgoodink.com/press

Chapter 4

1. Hegel, G. W. F. (1830/1975). *Lectures on the philosophy of world history. Introduction: Reason in history, second draft* (H.B. Nisbet, Trans.). Cambridge: Cambridge University Press
2. de Heer, C. (1969 A Study of the Semantic Field Denoting Happiness in Ancient Greek to the End of the Fifth Century B.C. Amsterdam: Adolf M. Hakkert
3. e-History (n.d.). Ancient history: 12,000 BC to 500 AD

timeline. Retrieved from http://www.dictionary.com/browse/luck.

4. McMahon, D.M. (2010). A History of happiness: We've forgotten much of what older traditions knew about happiness. Retrieved from http://www.yesmagazine.org/happiness/a-history-of-happiness.

5. McMahon, D.M. (2006). *Happiness: A history*. New York: Grove Press

6. Kraut, R. (2018, summer). Aristotle's ethics. In Edward N. Zalta (ed.). *The Stanford Encyclopedia of Philosophy* Retrieved from http://plato.stanford.edu/archives/spr2012/entries/aristotle-ethics/.

7. Burckhardt, J. (1914). *The civilization of the Renaissance in Italy*. New York: Macmillan.

8. Twoop (2005). Bubonic plague tmeline. Retrieved from http://www.twoop.com/medicine/archives/2005/10/bubonic_plague.html.

9. The Avalon Project (n.d.). *Declaration of the Rights of Man – 1789*. Retrieved from http://avalon.law.yale.edu/18th_century/rightsof.asp.

10. Miller, R. J. (2006). *Native America, discovered and conquered: Thomas Jefferson, Lewis & Clark, and manifest destiny*. Jersey: Greenwood Publishing Group.

11. Merk, F., & Merk, L. B. (1963). *Manifest destiny and mission in American history: A reinterpretation*. Cambridge, MA: Harvard University Press.

12. Durayappah-Harrison, A. (2010). What science has to say about genuine vs. fake smiles. Retrieved from http://www.psychologytoday.com/blog/thriving101/201001/what-science-has-say-about-genuine-vs-fake-smiles.

13. Layton, J (n.d.) Does smiling make you happy? Retrieved from http://tlc.howstuffworks.com/family/smiling-happy.htm.

14. Popular Songs Sung By The Soldiers, World War One Music & Songs (blog), http://www.ww1photos.com/WW-1MusicIndex.html.

15. Mandy Barrow to Britain Since the 1930s, Songs during the War (blog), http://www.primaryhomeworkhelp.co.uk/Britain.html.
16. Kent, W. & Burton, N. (1941). *White cliffs of Dover* [Recorded by Lynn, V.} Retrieved from http://www.songfacts.com/detail.php?lyrics=6727.
17. Kiger, P. (2011). How the American Dream works. Retrieved from http://people.howstuffworks.com/american-dream1.htm
18. BBC News (2011). Hundreds of Occupy Wall Street protesters arrested. Retrieved from http://www.bbc.com/news/world-us-canada-15140671

Chapter 5

1. Rubin, G. (2007). How to be happier: know yourself. harder than it sounds. Retrieved from http://happiness-project.com/happiness_project/2009/04/how-to-be-happier-know-yourself/
2. LeDoux, J. E. (2003). *Synaptic self: How our brains become who we are.* New York: Penguin Group

Chapter 6

1. Marano, H.E. (2003). Depression doing the thinking. Retrieved from http://www.psychologytoday.com/articles/200308/depression-doing-the-thinking.
2. Moore, M (2009). 7 Ways to leave negative self-talk behind. Retrieved from http://www.psychologytoday.com/blog/life-changes/200908/7-ways-leave-negative-self-talk-behind

Chapter 7

1. Steele, A. (n.d.). Extrinsic rewards. Retrieved from https://sites.google.com/site/motivationataglanceischool/

extrinsic-rewards.

2. Pink, D. H. (2011). *Drive: The surprising truth about what motivates us.* New York: Penguin Group

3. Deci, E. L. (1971). Effects of externally mediated rewards on intrinsic motivation. *Journal of personality and Social Psychology, 18*(1), 105.

4. Waterman, A. S., Schwartz, S. J., & Conti, R. (2008). The implications of two conceptions of happiness (hedonic enjoyment and eudaimonia) for the understanding of intrinsic motivation. *Journal of Happiness Studies, 9*(1), 41-79.

Chapter 9

1. Hsu, J. (2008). The secrets of storytelling. *Scientific American Mind* 19(46) Doi:10.1038/scientificamerican-mind0808-46 (accessed May 5, 2009).

2. O'Brien, J., & Kollock, P. (2001). Meaning is negotiated through interaction. In O'Brien, J. (Ed.) *The Production of reality: essays and readings on social interaction* (pp. 189-205). Thousand Oaks Ca: Pine Forge Press

3. Argyle, M. (2001). *The psychology of happiness.* New York: Routledge

4. Fowler, J. H., & Christakis, N. A. (2008). Dynamic spread of happiness in a large social network: longitudinal analysis over 20 years in the Framingham Heart Study. *BMJ* 337, a2338. Retrieved from http://www.bmj.com/content/337/bmj.a2338.full

5. Christakis, N. A. & Fowler, J. H., (2008). Social networks and happiness. Retrieved from http://www.edge.org/3rd_culture/christakis_fowler08/christakis_fowler08_index.html.

6. Colbert, S. (2010, January 7). *James Fowler. The Colbert Report* [Television broadcast]]. New York City: Spartina Productions

7. Christakis, N. A. & Fowler, J. H., (2008). Social net-

works and happiness. Retrieved from http://www.edge. org/3rd_culture/christakis_fowler08/christakis_fowler08_ index.html.

8. Lim, C., & Putnam, R. D. (2010). Religion, social networks, and life satisfaction. *American sociological review*, 75(6), 914-933.

9. Sohn, E. (2010). Why are religious people happier? Retrieved from https://www.livescience.com/9090-religion-people-happier-hint-god.html.

10. Moeller, P. (2012). How to find happiness on social networks. Retrieved from https://money.usnews.com/money/personal-finance/articles/2012/03/16/how-to-find-happiness-on-social-networks

11. Borgonovi, F. (2008). Doing well by doing good. The relationship between formal volunteering and self-reported health and happiness. *Social Science & Medicine*, 66(11), 2321-2334

Chapter 10

1.Carnegie Mellon University. (2006, November 8). Happy People Are Healthier, Psychologist Says. *ScienceDaily*. Retrieved May 7, 2018 from www.sciencedaily.com/releases/2006/11/061108103655.htm

Chapter 11

1. Bruner, J. (1991). The narrative construction of reality. *Critical inquiry*, 18(1), 1-21.

Chapter 12

1. Handy, D. (Producer), & Shadyac, T. (Director). 2010. *I Am* [Documentary]. (2011). Los Angeles, CA: Homemade Canvas Productions/Shady Acres.

www.ingramcontent.com/pod-product-compliance
Lightning Source LLC
Chambersburg PA
CBHW021931040426
42448CB00008B/1014